T0285846

Advance Praise

"Most of us navigate our private joys and woes without thinking about collective nuclear annihilation. This is not because the threat has vanished. It is because it is unthinkable. In this compelling work of rational doomsaying, Dupuy models how to think the unthinkable. The result is a challenging and urgent book."
—Alison McQueen, author of *Political Realism in Apocalyptic Times*

"This is a provocative exploration of the paradoxes of nuclear deterrence. If we are to postpone nuclear catastrophe indefinitely, Dupuy argues, we must understand that nuclear war is not merely possible but bound to occur."
—David Holloway, author of *Stalin and the Bomb*

"We all live under the shadow of a forthcoming catastrophe: pandemic, ecological disaster, nuclear war. . . . Our reactions to such threats are often irrational, and Dupuy provides a superbly readable rational analysis of all these irrationalities: why the logic of nuclear MAD (mutually assured destruction) is really mad, why nuclear threats are never just rhetoric but can trigger an actual catastrophe, why sometimes to be taken seriously one has to act as if one is mad, why the only rational strategy is to accept that things can at any moment go wrong. . . . Dupuy is our best theorist of catastrophes and his new book is a book for all of us—in a well-organized state, it would be massively printed and freely distributed to all families. So it is vulgar and trivial to say that this is an excellent book—it is rather a book that we all need like ordinary daily bread."
—Slavoj Žižek, author of *Surplus-Enjoyment*

"Dupuy provides an extremely important service by bringing much-needed attention to the existential risk that society largely ignored prior to the war in Ukraine and, even now, does not take seriously enough. Highly recommended."
—Martin E. Hellman, winner of the Turing Award

"Dupuy, one of the most incisive thinkers of our times, allows us to rethink history while it is in the making. This book is mandatory reading for anyone who seeks to understand our present."
—Frank Ruda, coauthor of *Reading Hegel*

"A stimulating read, essential for understanding the remaining options afforded to our civilization, now that we live with the irreversibility of the nuclear bomb."
—Diane Delaurens, *Nonfiction*

The War That Must Not Occur

The War That Must Not Occur

Jean-Pierre Dupuy

Translated by
Malcolm DeBevoise

STANFORD UNIVERSITY PRESS
Stanford, California

Stanford University Press
Stanford, California

The War That Must Not Occur was originally published in French in 2019 under the title *La guerre qui ne peut pas avoir lieu* © 2019, Groupe Elidia Éditions Desclée de Brouwer, 10, rue Mercoeur—75011 Paris / 9, espace Méditerranée—66000 Perpignan www.editionsddb.fr

Support for this translation was provided by Imitatio, a project of the Thiel Foundation.

Printed in the United States of America on acid-free, archival-quality paper

Cataloging-in-Publication Data available upon request.
Library of Congress Control Number: 2022051118
ISBN: 9781503635159 (cloth), 9781503636651 (ebook)

Cover designer: Martyn Schmoll
Text designer: Elliott Beard

I've always thought about the issue of nuclear war; it's a very important element in my thought process. It's the ultimate, the ultimate catastrophe, the biggest problem this world has, and nobody's focusing on the nuts and bolts of it. It's a little like sickness. People don't believe they're going to get sick until they do. Nobody wants to talk about it. I believe the greatest of all stupidities is people's believing it will never happen, because everyone knows how destructive it will be, so nobody uses weapons. What bullshit.

DONALD TRUMP
1 March 1990

Contents

Introduction

This book is about nuclear warfare. As a philosopher, I have pondered the implications of this nightmarish scenario for twenty years, without claiming to be either an expert or a specialist. More generally, I have thought about the history and philosophy of violence since encountering the work of René Girard in the late 1970s. This inevitably led me to consider catastrophes and the problem of evil, particularly in relation to the threats to the future of humanity posed by climate change, the risk that advanced technologies—nanobiotechnologies, synthetic biology, human genome editing, and the like—may escape the control of their inventors, and, not least, nuclear war. Nuclear war has furnished me with a template for a form of rational doomsaying that describes a relationship to the future that I call projected time. This conception of time implies that once what is at risk is monumental, beyond all human measure, it is legitimate to hold that catastrophic events, once they become possible, are bound to occur. Here possibility implies necessity. The difficult thing to understand is that this necessity in no way amounts to fatalism. It may be within our power, as I show in this book, to postpone catastrophe ad vitam aeternam. Nevertheless, we must regard catastrophe as necessary; otherwise our wanting to delay its occurrence would not be sufficiently motivated. If catastrophe is merely possible, then its non-occurrence is equally possible. It is not a contradiction, in other words, to believe in both the necessity of the future and its indeterminacy.

The problem of nuclear warfare leads us to reformulate some of the most important and most difficult questions of metaphysics.[1] A reliance on abstraction and a priori reasoning becomes unavoidable in the light of a very simple and quite stunning fact. Thomas Schelling, whose writings on the mathematical theory of games have had a great influence on nuclear doctrines, memorably referred to it at the beginning of his lecture in Stockholm in December 2005 on being awarded the Nobel Prize in Economic Sciences: "The most spectacular event of the past half century is one that did not occur. We have enjoyed sixty years without nuclear weapons being exploded in anger." More than fifteen years later, this observation still holds. Schelling's opening words are often recalled, but what he said next has for the most part been forgotten: "In 1960 the British novelist C. P. Snow said on the first page of the *New York Times* that unless the nuclear powers drastically reduced their nuclear armaments thermonuclear war within the decade was a 'mathematical certainty.'[2] Nobody seemed to think Snow's statement extravagant."[3] The coupling here of necessity and indeterminacy is a paradox well worth reflecting upon.

The situations and events that I review here and in the first two chapters of this book were selected mainly for the purpose of illustrating the concepts analyzed in the final two chapters. Most of what has been written and said about the Ukrainian crisis, for instance, comes almost exclusively under the head of geopolitics. This dimension is essential, but it is by no means the only one that needs to be taken into account. Nuclear war has its own syntax, which is superimposed on the intentions and decisions of world leaders. Putin's psychology no doubt plays a role in the present instance, just as Trump's did during the North Korean crisis. Nor can the importance of Ukraine in Russian history and culture be neglected, any more than the role played by the United States in the military

command structure of NATO can be. But when a potentially nuclear confrontation begins to escalate, these so-called actors look
more like marionettes, driven this way and that by forces beyond
their control, even if these are forces of their own making. They still
believe that they are in control, of course, that violence obeys their
will, but the truth is otherwise: violence manipulates them according to its own laws.

   It is this aspect of the matter I am concerned with in the present
book. The Ukrainian crisis is only a particular case study. Nevertheless, I hasten to take advantage of the opportunity to introduce
the book to an American audience in order to sketch the outlines of
an analysis of the events taking place today in accordance with the
method I develop in the pages that follow.

Most people, except French experts and others who claim that the
current crisis cannot possibly lead to a nuclear conflict amounting
to a third world war, anxiously wonder what the chances[4] are of
this scenario coming to pass. Will Putin drop an atomic bomb on a
Ukrainian city in order to make Zelensky surrender? Scott Sagan,
a prominent authority, thinks it is by no means an implausible
outcome. The United States did just this, he reminds us, in order
to force Japan's surrender in 1945.[5] Will the Russian president go
so far as to target a European capital in order to punish NATO for
providing Ukraine with increasingly powerful and sophisticated
weapons? Given Russia's quantitative superiority, is he prepared
to launch intercontinental ballistic missiles against the only other
great nuclear power, the United States?

   At this juncture we need to consider a prior question, the one
that Schelling raised in his Nobel lecture: how are we to explain
the fact that since 9 August 1945, the date of Nagasaki's decimation,
no atomic bomb has been dropped on civilian populations with the
aim of exterminating them? If we knew the answer to this question,
we might be in a position to estimate the chance that this mysteri-
ous blessing will continue to favor us—as though there were a good
fairy who watches over humanity and prevents it from destroying
itself.

Why should the unprecedented power of the atomic bomb not be a sufficient reason to dissuade anyone from even thinking of using it? Isn't the principle of deterrence entailed, as a matter of practical reason, by its immeasurable destructiveness? Who could possibly have an interest in escalating a conflict to the point that there are no winners, only losers? These questions have been with us since 1945, and they remain no less perplexing today. Attempts were made during the Cold War to reduce both the power of atomic weapons and the range of the missiles that carry them in the hope of bringing the devastation produced by a nuclear conflict nearer to that which a traditional war is capable of producing. Eventually it became clear, however, that these so-called tactical weapons and missiles must be banned. Their relatively small explosive force[6] encourages military planners to use them on the battlefield, as in the case of conventional weapons, with the risk of getting caught up in a nuclear spiral whose inevitable tendency, as can be shown by a priori reasoning, is to spin out of control and lead to mutual annihilation. Just as the explosion of an atomic bomb triggers the thermonuclear reaction within a hydrogen bomb, so too the use of tactical nuclear weapons on the battlefield is the surest way for intercontinental ballistic missiles to be brought out from their silos, notwithstanding that these missiles are supposed, by virtue of their passive existence alone, to assure nuclear peace.

This explanation in terms of interests—the interests of each person and the interest of all—nonetheless runs up against the sobering lessons of our own time. The tragedy of human history is that very often it destroys the very people who make it, even though each one of them tries only to satisfy his or her own interests. Tactical nuclear weapons were in fact banned for a time, at least partially, as we will see. Today, however, they are more numerous than ever.

An entirely different explanation for the absence of nuclear war is that we narrowly escaped it; chance and purely chance—that is to say, luck—has spared us the worst. Historians of the nuclear era record many incidents that could have set off a fatal escalation but did not: miscommunication among key figures, errors of interpretation, rash calculations of risk, fits of rage, and so on. In each case horror only just missed becoming reality. I examine several such episodes. The relative weakness of the explanation from luck has to do with the fact that we do not know whether chance was responsible for the incident that threatened disaster or whether it was because of chance that disaster was averted. For want of a common preternatural cause for this series of near catastrophes, it is reasonable to suppose that one day luck will grow tired of the coin always coming up heads and that the moment will inevitably come when it will come up tails—not least because this should have happened long ago.

The simplest, most obvious, and most common explanation is that it is because deterrence has succeeded that nuclear war was able to be prevented. On this view, the possession of an atomic arsenal has only one aim: to dissuade other nuclear powers from attacking first, by threatening them with disproportionate retaliation if they pay no heed and, if need be, by extending this threat to a nonnuclear attack that would imperil the nation's vital interests. A good part of the present book is devoted to discussing this claim. Once again, what makes it a genuine philosophical puzzle is the lack of empirical evidence and the corresponding need to resort to a priori reasoning.

Many philosophers and strategists have concluded that deterrence can work only if each of the leaders of two rival nuclear powers has reason to believe that the other is irrational.[7] The chief obstacle to nuclear deterrence is that the threat of retaliation on which it depends is not credible. If deterrence fails, will the nation that has been attacked really carry out its threat and unleash a suicidal escalation? Does one have to be mad, or pretend to be mad, in order to be credible? The soundness of deterrence turns on the answer to this question.

Whatever the answer may be, a major reason to doubt that deterrence is mainly responsible for the absence of nuclear war for almost eighty years now is that it has seldom actually been practiced. In its pure form, deterrence requires giving up the very thing that gives armed forces their legitimacy: the power to defend. By making it clear to an adversary that you will do nothing to stop any missiles that it may launch against you—for example, by means of an antiballistic missile shield—your adversary can be assured that you will not attack first. For if you were to launch a first strike, that would not prevent your adversary from carrying out the threat of a ruinous reprisal by virtue of its capacity to launch a second strike. In that case no one attacks first, and what is called a balance of terror (or, a remarkable oxymoron, nuclear peace) is in principle realized. But the abandonment by the armed forces of their primary mission, to defend the nation from attack, is not a price they are prepared to pay. I analyze several striking cases where the principle of deterrence has been disregarded altogether.

What purpose have nuclear weapons served, then, if they are only remotely associated with the absence of nuclear war? Paradoxically, they have made the possibility of a first strike more likely. In making the first move ("preemptively," in the jargon of nuclear strategists), one side responds to a potential attack as if it had already taken place. The answer comes before the question—thus the temporal inversion that forms the leitmotif of this book: retaliation in advance. Whatever their official nuclear doctrines may say to the contrary, a first strike has never been ruled out by either Soviet (later Russian) or American leaders. Nevertheless, convincing an adversary that one is prepared to strike first is no less problematic than convincing an adversary that one will forcefully respond to its attack. Here again the problem of credibility arises. A first strike will not be sufficient to neutralize an enemy who retains the capacity to retaliate. It is therefore necessary to make the enemy believe that you will be able to absorb a retaliatory strike while limiting the damage from it—which is to say that you will remain fully capable of retaliating against retaliation. That may be very difficult to do.

The United States and Russia have had, and continue to have, an ambivalent attitude toward an element of nuclear doctrine known, misleadingly, as "escalate to de-escalate." Their vacillation in this regard illustrates a dilemma facing both of them in respect of deterrence and preemption that has a direct bearing on the Ukrainian crisis. The idea of escalating in order to de-escalate, introduced by Schelling in *The Strategy of Conflict* (1960), has influenced several generations of strategists. The doctrine of flexible response formulated by Robert McNamara shortly afterward and the concepts of limited nuclear war, escalation control, and the like are so many variations on the same theme. The simplest way to think about it is to compare it to the logic of an auction, where one keeps pushing the price up until the other bidders drop out. Similarly, one increases the intensity of combat with nonnuclear (conventional) forces until resort to a nuclear strike seems inevitable in order to end the conflict by forcing the enemy to yield. This is what is called de-escalation.

I advance a number of arguments showing not only the vacuousness of this idea but also the dangers that are bound to follow if it is put into effect. Carl von Clausewitz was perhaps the first to point out, in *On War* (1832), that as a theoretical matter there is no decisive move that will put a halt to an increasingly violent sequence of events. More often than not, Clausewitz observed, logistical and other obstacles—what he called the fog of war—combine to prevent mutual annihilation from coming to pass. In the case of nuclear war, by contrast, these same obstacles accelerate an escalation to extremes.

Both American and Russian nuclear strategists recite the credo of nuclear deterrence: a limited attack cannot be deterred by making a threat of limited retaliation credible; it can be deterred only by sustaining a moderate probability of mutual annihilation. In practice, however, the fact remains that the option of escalating to de-escalate continues to tempt military planners, particularly on the Russian side, so far as we can judge from unofficial public statements. According to Alexei Arbatov, a senior national security advisor, "Conventional precision weapons should be capable of inflicting sufficient losses on attacking NATO forces and bases to induce NATO either to stop its aggression, or to escalate it to the level of massive conventional warfare, including a ground offensive. This *would then justify* Russia's first use of tactical nuclear weapons."[8]

From the point of view of deterrence, this can be seen only as an admission of failure. The fact that we have escaped a third world war involving strategic nuclear weapons, even that no atomic weapon of limited power has yet been used under battlefield conditions, seems nothing short of a miracle. In order to provide a satisfactory explanation for this extraordinary state of affairs—what Schelling called an event that did not occur—it will be necessary to rely on a negative form of metaphysical argument, after the example of negative (or apophatic) theology. For the moment, however, we know enough to be able to venture an answer to the question that concerns us here, namely, whether it is possible that the Ukrainian crisis will lead to nuclear war and, if so, what is the likelihood of this happening.

On 1 February and 2 February 2019 two things happened that went largely unnoticed by world public opinion and that in large measure account for the present state of affairs. First Trump and then Putin the next day announced that their countries intended to withdraw from the treaty signed more than thirty years earlier, in 1987, by Ronald Reagan and Mikhail Gorbachev, who thereby agreed to eliminate from their respective nuclear arsenals all ground-launched cruise missiles and ballistic missiles with ranges of between 500 and 5,500 kilometers (310 and 3,420 miles). The Intermediate-Range Nuclear Forces (INF) Treaty was a misnomer, for the accord did not limit nuclear forces per se. It banned a certain class of missiles, whether they were equipped with nuclear warheads or not. The American withdrawal took effect on 2 August 2019.

It will be instructive to recall the historical background to this joint decision. For more than ten years, between 1976 and 1987, the Euromissile crisis aroused enormous fear and controversy in European nations. In March 1976, the Soviet Union deployed in its western region SS20 missiles having a range of about 5,000 kilometers, capable therefore of reaching not only Western Europe but also China and Japan. The American president, Jimmy Carter, felt confident, in accordance with the accepted principles of deterrence, that America's long-range strategic nuclear weapons sufficed to discourage the Soviet Union from launching a surprise attack on Europe. But the West German chancellor, Helmut Schmidt, urged the United States to intervene directly. In December 1979, at a summit of NATO leaders, it was decided to enter into negotiations aimed at forcing the Soviet Union to withdraw its SS20s and, if these talks failed, to install Pershing II medium-range missiles in West Germany within four years.

There followed a confused period that survives in popular memory today mainly in the form of slogans. The German pacifists, supported by the French Communist Party, declared that they would rather be "red than dead," to which François Mitterrand replied that "the pacifists are in the West and the missiles are in the East." As it turns out, the Pershing IIs were deployed in West Germany on schedule, in November 1983. Shortly thereafter the geopolitical situation completely changed with the coming to power of Mikhail Gorbachev in March 1985. He and Reagan met in Reykjavik a year and a half later, in October 1986, and came close to reaching an agreement in principle on a general disarmament. I discuss the reasons for the summit's failure in chapter 2. Détente had nonetheless been established and led in the following year to the INF Treaty, signed on 8 December 1987. It is this treaty that Trump and Putin repudiated in February 2019.

To no one's surprise, the two leaders accused each other of bad faith. Both could plausibly argue that the other nation had long been in violation of the INF Treaty. Trump, it has been said, had no policy in any area that did not consist merely in undoing what Barack Obama had done before him, but in this regard at least he was a worthy successor. In 2014, the Obama administration had become alarmed by Russian deployment of a cruise missile system that in every respect resembled the kind banned by the INF Treaty. The Russians had begun testing this system long before, however, in 2008, while making no attempt to hide what they were doing; indeed, Putin openly complained five years later that whereas Russia was constrained by the treaty, it was surrounded in Asia by countries that were free to equip themselves with medium-range nuclear weapons, most notably China. The United States, after much indecision, concluded that it had no satisfactory response under the existing regime and declared the treaty dead.

Meanwhile, Russia accused America of cheating—for example, by taking the liberty of installing ballistic missile defense systems in Eastern Europe. Apart from the fact that they violated the ABM Treaty, these shields could easily be converted into offensive weapons. Furthermore, armed drones, which can be adapted to the same purpose as missiles, did not exist in 1987.

NATO, for its part, declared that Russia was wholly to blame for violating the treaty and, more than this, that the treaty was not worth saving—a strange position, endorsed by France, since it was in large measure thanks to this treaty that peace in Europe had been guaranteed and the security of NATO preserved for more than thirty years. In a nuclear world, however, where rationality is indistinguishable from madness, it is not necessary to separate the good from the wicked.

It is against this background that the most recent events are to be seen, including Putin's decision to invade Ukraine while threatening anyone who might stand in his way with nuclear annihilation. The relative military strength of Russia and the United States needs to be taken into consideration as well. The end of the Cold War brought about a spectacular reversal in the balance of power between Washington and Moscow in terms of their respective shares of nuclear and conventional weapons. Before 1989, the Soviet Union's superiority in conventional weapons was manifest, and the United States had sought to compensate for this disadvantage by building up its nuclear arsenal. After the collapse of the USSR, the Pentagon turned its attention elsewhere, particularly to regional conflicts for which conventional weapons were better suited than atomic bombs. During this same period, Putin built up Russia's nuclear arsenal.

It was not nuclear warfare in general that the United States neglected, but tactical nuclear warfare. American doctrine called for conventional weapons to be used in regional conflicts and, in the event that escalation for the purpose of de-escalation became necessary, reliance on strategic nuclear weapons delivered by ICBMs. Today the United States has only a hundred or so tactical nuclear warheads in Europe, distributed between Germany, the Netherlands, Belgium, Italy, and Turkey. Russia has perhaps twenty times this many, a substantial number of them based in the exclave wedged between Poland and Lithuania (a strategic place if ever there was one) known as the Kaliningrad Oblast—a tragic historical irony, since Immanuel Kant wrote *Perpetual Peace* (1795) in the capital of this region, known as Königsberg when it was part of Prussia; the parents of Hannah Arendt, who wrote *The Origins of Totalitarianism* (1951), were from here as well.

Putin is evidently proud of the superiority of his tactical nuclear arsenal, which is what matters in the present instance. More disturbing still, he believes that Russia is better prepared than the United States to ride out a nuclear exchange between the two countries. We have seen that this is the condition of a successful preemptive strike—that is, of successfully attacking first.

Given this much, how did the two nuclear superpowers react to their mutual rejection of the INF Treaty in 2019? Recall that this agreement imposed limits on missiles, whether they carry nuclear weapons or not. The United States and NATO immediately seized the opportunity that now presented itself of stationing nonnuclear intermediate-range and shorter-range missiles in Europe. But they failed to reckon with the Russian response, repeated several times, calling upon the United States and NATO to impose a moratorium on the deployment in Europe of missiles equipped with nuclear warheads. This demand has remained a dead letter. Emmanuel Macron, while categorically refusing to accept it, raised a pertinent question: "Has the absence of dialogue with Russia made the European continent any safer? I don't think so."[9]

Here, one point of technical detail has considerable importance. It is impossible to determine whether or not a ballistic missile is carrying a nuclear warhead until it reaches its target. Faced with this indeterminacy, Russia has elected to treat any missile approaching its territory as evidence of a nuclear attack. According to official doctrine, this is reason enough for Russia to launch its own nuclear missiles even before enemy missiles land on its soil—forcing the United States, which had thought it had a free hand once more to deploy both conventional and nuclear missiles in Europe, to think again. All this, it needs to be kept in mind, took place in the months leading up to Putin's invasion of Ukraine.

In the first chapter of this book I consider a similar case, the upshot of which is that, in the nuclear age, it is necessary to treat all alerts produced by early warning systems, whether true or false, as though they were true. This is an essential property of the theory of apocalyptic prophecy that I argue for here: once a major catastrophe appears to be possible, one must assume that it is going to occur. In the case of the war in Ukraine, as in all others of its kind, the rule is this: given several possible outcomes, it is necessary to concentrate on the worst one, however great or small the degree of its future necessity[10]—and this in order to prevent it from occurring.

I am aware that I have not answered the question that is uppermost in everyone's mind. Will Putin launch nuclear missiles against a Ukrainian or a European city? As philosophers often do, I have reformulated it. This apocalyptic scenario is evidently a possibility, since nothing stands in the way of an error or some unlucky accident precipitating catastrophe, whether due to "noise" in the system, a miscommunication, or the diabolical cycle of humiliation that creates resentment and then causes it to be acted on. It needs to be assumed, as I say, that the worst is going to occur, and, for just this reason, everything that can be done must be done to ensure that it will not occur.

The French president was certainly imprudent in saying, as he did on 3 June 2022, that Russia must not be humiliated.[11] This was interpreted in psychological and moral terms, as if to say, shockingly, that due attention needed to be paid to the feelings of the aggressor. Instead Macron should have said that the world is at the mercy of the whims of one of its leaders, meaning that the international system is structurally unstable—an academic way of saying extremely fragile.

My analysis almost completely neglects the geopolitical aspect of the question. I do not by any means wish to minimize its importance. My purpose in what follows is simply to demonstrate the decisive power of the instrument of destruction employed: an atomic weapon. The instrument is not neutral; whether it brings about good or evil does not depend on the intentions of those who make use of it. Not long ago America mourned for the victims of a mass shooting that took the lives of nineteen children who were scarcely ten years old. The killer was eighteen years old. From this latest episode, a good many Americans concluded that access to firearms should be expanded rather than limited. Violence is needed to cast out violence. Violence alone, it is believed, can protect against the mental illness and radical malignancy of others. Whoever makes this argument is blind to the quasi-autonomy of decision that firearms have acquired. It is as though possessing them means giving up one's free will. Likewise, as I trust this book will demonstrate, the mere possession of nuclear weapons is a moral abomination.

24 January 2023

One

Ninety Seconds from Apocalypse
and Why (Almost) No One Gives a Damn

> Today, the danger of some sort of nuclear catastrophe is
> greater than it was during the Cold War, and most people
> are blissfully unaware of this danger.
>
> WILLIAM J. PERRY
> *My Journey at the Nuclear Brink (2015)*

The Apocalypse That Did Not Occur

On Saturday, 13 January 2018, the world came within an inch of
nuclear war and no one knew it—apart from a few million people in
the Hawaiian Islands. That day, inhabitants and tourists alike were
terror-stricken for thirty-eight very long minutes. They all felt sure
they were going to die. They had the terrible sense of being trapped;
there seemed to be no way of escaping the imminent horror. At 8:07
a.m., everyone with a cell phone or access to the Internet received
this warning: "BALLISTIC[1] MISSILE THREAT INBOUND TO
HAWAII. SEEK IMMEDIATE SHELTER. THIS IS NOT A DRILL."

Note the last sentence. In a society saturated with "fake news,"
it seemed essential to make it clear that the announcement of a
nuclear attack was not a false alert, even if only a few minutes remained before the missiles arrived. But there is no guarantee that

an alert claiming not to be false is in fact true, since a false alert mas-
querading as an authentic warning—a hoax, for example, on a grand
scale à la Orson Welles[2]—would also deny that it is a simulation.
When Magritte painted a pipe in a thoroughly realistic fashion and
wrote below it, "This is not a pipe," one might have supposed that he
meant to emphasize the difference between the representation of an
object and the object itself. But the inscription that appears on the
painting is falsified within the domain of representation—that is, by
the painting itself—because what is represented is well and truly a
pipe.[3] A logician would say that the truth value of the proposition
"This alert is not a false alert," like that of "This is not a pipe," is
indeterminate. As we will see, indeterminacy is the key to what is
called the balance of terror.

We now have very vivid and terrifying recollections of the
manner in which this indeterminacy was experienced during the
nearly forty minutes before state officials announced that the alert
really was a false alert. The exact nature of the error remains un-
clear. At the first it was thought that an employee of the Hawaii
Emergency Management Agency had clicked on the wrong button
without realizing it. Later it became known that he had clicked on
the button that was the right one *from his point of view*, for he hon-
estly believed that an attack was imminent.[4] The exact nature of the
error is important insofar as it concerns his personal culpability,
but, as we will see, it has no bearing on the lessons to be drawn from
this incident.

What does one think about when one believes that one has only
a few minutes to live before being transformed into a shadow in the
doorway of one's home—a ghastly image familiar in the aftermath
of the bombing of Hiroshima? Cynthia Lazaroff and Bruce Allyn, a
couple living on the island of Kauai (the oldest of the Hawaiian ar-
chipelago), gave a deeply moving account. The one a filmmaker and
the other a scholar, both specializing in U.S.-Russian relations, they
had spent the year 2017 interviewing a great many senior officials
and experts for the purpose of evaluating the risks of an escalation
leading to nuclear war.[5] Faced with a practical application of their
research, it was as though they had forgotten everything. Their

minds were paralyzed by fear. Today they know the questions they should have asked themselves but only caught fleeting glimpses of, as in a dream. Where did the missiles come from? Were they launched by Kim Jong Un or Putin? This was not an academic question: depending on the answer, the time they had left to live might be very different. If the missiles came from North Korea, about twenty to twenty-five minutes; if from Russia, what mattered was the delivery vehicle—missiles launched from a submarine might take even less time. And what was the target? Both Honolulu, the state capital, and Kauai were plausible candidates. The first because the city's port, Pearl Harbor, is the headquarters of the U.S. Pacific Fleet and because North Korea has shown an interest in it, perhaps for symbolic reasons; the second because it is on this island that the United States established the world's largest facility for testing antiballistic missiles, particularly ones meant to destroy missiles coming from North Korea.

Much more immediate questions presented themselves. Parents with adult children who lived nearby faced a tragic dilemma, having to decide which one they would spend their last moments with. For some people, the problem was finding shelter. How to arrange to meet up with friends and family? Out of habit, people who left their homes locked the doors—as if the chance of being robbed while they were gone was anything to worry about under the circumstances. The highways were filled with terrified drivers crashing into one another at speeds of more than 100 mph. A disaster film. Only it wasn't a film; it was reality.

Most officials and elected representatives have already forgotten all this. No lesson has been drawn: an apocalypse that did not happen, nothing more. The poor fellow who sent out the false alert provided a convenient scapegoat. The remedy was simple: redundancy. Assign supervisors to each emergency management agency employee. But there had been other such incidents in the past, and there will be others in the future. Three days later, the same scenario played out in Japan, mistakenly thought to be in imminent danger of a strike by a North Korean missile. This time the error was corrected in five minutes.

In such cases American military vocabulary speaks of a "near miss." Interestingly, this expression says the opposite of what it is supposed to mean, as if an attacker had missed the target it was aiming at. Instead, one should speak of a "near hit"—the ultimate horror was avoided, but only just. An alert issued by the U.S. military command leaves the president five or ten minutes to decide whether to launch a battery of intercontinental ballistic missiles before they are destroyed in their silos. If the alert is false but the order to fire has been given, then a third world war has been triggered. Any war after that, as Einstein observed, would be fought with sticks and stones.

William Perry, to whom we are indebted for having survived more than one apocalypse that did not occur during his tenure as secretary of defense between 1994 and 1997 under Clinton, has drawn the correct conclusion from the Hawaiian incident: from now on, the nuclear era obliges us to take seriously every threat, no matter how outlandish, and to treat every alert, no matter how inaccurate, as if it were true.[6] The chief danger today does not come from the malign intentions of the leaders of nuclear powers. None of them wish for war. It comes from what may generically be called an accident. This may be an error of strategic calculation, a misinterpretation of a statement made by the enemy, a fit of rage that incapacitates rational thought, a functionary who inadvertently presses the wrong button or clicks on the wrong link.[7] It does not matter which. A false alert, if it is not strategic, is itself an accident. What difference is there between missiles that actually strike California and a false alert that says missiles are approaching California if this false alert unleashes, in the form of a response exactly identical to the attack it was falsely believed to be responding to, a process that, as in the case of a true alert, will lead to what Carl von Clausewitz called an escalation to extremes—that is, mutual annihilation?[8]

From the point of view of a logician, then, the Kauai false alert asserted the proposition "This is not a simulation of apocalypse." The indeterminacy of this proposition, which we noted earlier, is what Perry had in mind in warning that nuclear alerts, whatever their actual truth value may be, must be treated *as though* they are accurate. The Hawaiian incident was *an apocalypse that did not occur*. It may be that, looking to the future, whatever reason we have for hope lies in just this possibility: that the worst need not come to pass.

War and Deterrence

In a sinister way the Hawaiian incident belatedly marked the end of the annus horribilis of 2017, which in retrospect appears to have been a tipping point. Up until then, the key concept in thinking about nuclear war was deterrence. In principle, deterrence converts the unimaginable power of atomic weapons into abject powerlessness, because the weapons are unused. The relation of deterrence to war is paradoxical. Deterrence consists in threatening war: war that is deferred, adjourned, delayed; war that is waged by means of words and signs—in short, war that does not take place.[9] This should remind us of the rituals of traditional societies, where, in order to say that one will not make war, one imitates it; on the verge of actually committing violence, one steps back, at the very edge of the precipice. It is a question of making it clear that one could make war, while at the last moment stopping short of it. In the context of deterrence, French nuclear strategy uses the image of a tightrope, a rope that is pulled taut to the breaking point. The image of a precipice is preferred in English, and the word associated with it, brinkmanship,[10] has become one of the basic concepts of American strategy.

In 2017 everything changed. As in Chuck Jones's Road Runner cartoons, Donald Trump and Kim Jong Un went over the edge while still managing somehow to remain standing on thin air, the abyss beneath them. During the summer of that year, fears began to grow that the escalation of words between the two leaders had reached such heights of insanity that only a reciprocal exchange of atomic strikes could calm their nerves, at the price of millions dead. Nuclear war was now thought to be possible, even probable, not only with North Korea but also with China and Russia; two prominent American experts put the odds at between 20 and 50 percent.[11] In its 27 January 2018 issue, featuring a special report titled "The Next

War," *The Economist* reckoned that war was a "real possibility," while arguing that containing and deterring North Korea remained the best policy. Several months earlier, writing in *Foreign Affairs*, Scott Sagan, a leading authority on international security, declared that "the risk that an accident, a false warning, or a misperceived military exercise could lead to a war is alarmingly high," concluding that "the current Korean missile crisis is even more dangerous than the Cuban one."[12] Sagan agreed that deterrence continued to be the best option, with the United States and the world accepting North Korea's right to maintain a nuclear arsenal and even to expand it.

In response to this state of affairs, at the beginning of January 2018, the editors of *The Bulletin of the Atomic Scientists* moved the minute hand of the Doomsday Clock forward by thirty seconds, to two minutes before midnight—midnight being, by convention, the moment when humanity will have thrown itself into the fiery cauldron of nuclear oblivion. The Doomsday Clock was created in 1947 by a group of physicists who considered the bombing of Hiroshima and Nagasaki to have been indefensible and were determined to monitor future research and development associated with the ultimate weapon of mass destruction. They founded the *Bulletin* that same year, setting the minute hand of the clock at seven minutes before midnight. This was the beginning of the nuclear era. Since then the minute hand has been moved forward and back some twenty times. Until recently the closest it had come to midnight, two minutes, was in 1953, when the United States and the Soviet Union tested a hydrogen bomb within nine months of each other. After the fall of the Berlin Wall, the collapse of the Soviet Union, and the end of the Cold War, it was put back to seventeen minutes and then advanced to seven minutes before midnight again with the terrorist attacks of 11 September 2001. In the judgment of the clock's custodians, since January 24, 2023, we find ourselves in a situation worse than the worst moment of the Cold War: we are now ninety seconds from midnight. The fact that the country with the largest nuclear arsenal now threatens the countries of NATO with annihilation is not the least of the reasons for this.

The Trump Case

Donald Trump was not always the man he became as president of the United States of the America. The words I have borrowed as an epigraph for the present book, and which I could have written myself, except for the style, are proof of this. My ambition is to give a quasi-structuralist account of what it means to live with nuclear weapons. A person's psychology—even the psychology of someone who holds the highest office in the most powerful country in the world—is purely a matter of contingency. The French structuralists of the 1960s and 1970s hated psychology.[13] Here, however, it seems to me to be essential.

It would be a grave error to suppose that Trump was a cause, for he was above all a consequence. Trump's election was but a symptom of the advanced decay of American democracy.

To begin with, Trump was elected by chance. Here it will be useful to keep in mind Claude Lefort's profound insight concerning the institution of voting. "Nothing brings out the paradox of democracy more clearly," he wrote, "than universal suffrage. It is precisely at the moment when popular sovereignty is supposed to manifest itself, when the people are to be actualized by expressing their will, that social bonds are torn apart, that the citizen finds himself extracted from all the networks in which social life develops and converted into a unit of account. *Number is substituted for substance.*"[14]

The essential political act of a democracy, the choice of who will govern, is reduced to an exercise in vote counting, which entails the destruction of the very things that bind the members of society to one another. In the United States in 2016, considering numbers alone, the switch of a very small number of votes from one candidate to the other in five or six key states would have tipped the balance away from Trump in favor of Hillary Clinton. This is the modern definition of chance: small causes that produce large effects. The operation of chance in this sense is not uncommon in American presidential elections, and the effects are magnified by the fact that presidents are elected not by direct universal suffrage but through the intermediation of an electoral college. In the contest between

George W. Bush and Al Gore in 2000, for example, the popular vote was almost equally divided, with the difference between the ballots cast for each candidate proving to be smaller than what the devices used for recording and counting ballots were capable of accurately measuring.[15]

Trump's election came as a surprise; indeed, no one was more surprised than Trump himself. But that does not imply that his election was unmeaningful. To the contrary, it revealed a state of American society that would have remained hidden had Clinton won, chance once again having decided the matter.

Much has been said and written about Trump's narcissism, his breathtaking egocentricity, and so forth. I believe the matter is quite otherwise. Narcissism, as Freud defines it, is the outward expression of an ego that is full—full of itself, to the point of overflowing. Trump's ego is empty. This is why he craves the admiration, attention, and love of others, in order to fill himself up, like a vampire that slakes its thirst with the blood of its victims. This is why he experiences mockery and rejection as an intolerable humiliation and will not rest until he has made his critics pay for their insolence. In France, psychiatric nosology refers to perverse narcissism; in America, to Asperger's syndrome. Self-love? One should rather speak of self-hatred, thinking of Nietzsche's penetrating insight: "Whoever is dissatisfied with himself is continually ready for revenge, and we others will be his victims."[16]

But Trump's condition can be described more precisely with reference to the conception of evil that Jean-Jacques Rousseau called *amour-propre*, contrasting it with *amour de soi*, which characterizes the goodness of man in a state of nature. To be sure, these expressions are antiquated, but their pertinence has not been diminished by time. In the most extraordinary text he left us on the opposition between *amour-propre* and *amour de soi*, the *Dialogues* (also known under the title *Rousseau, Judge of Jean-Jacques*), Rousseau wrote:

> The primitive passions, which all tend directly toward our happiness, focus us only on objects that relate to it, and, having only *amour de soi* as a principle, are all loving and gentle in

their essence. But when, being deflected from their object by obstacles, they focus on removing the obstacle rather than on reaching the object, then they change nature and become irascible and hateful. And that is how *amour de soi*, which is a good and absolute feeling, becomes *amour-propre*, which is a relative feeling by which one makes comparisons; the latter feeling demands preferences, and its enjoyment is purely negative, as it no longer seeks satisfaction in our own benefit but solely in the harm of another.[17]

Let us concentrate our attention on this crucial passage: "When, being deflected from their object by obstacles, [the passions] focus on removing the obstacle rather than on reaching the object." How better to describe the jealous passion of someone who becomes so obsessed with a rival that he loses sight of the object he covets? From this fixation spring all the evils that fill Pandora's box, foremost among them envy, jealousy, and impotent hatred, to quote Stendhal. How better to describe the illness from which Trump suffers? One knows only too well that he flies into a rage over the most ridiculous things, very often illusory or untrue: the size of the crowd at his inauguration, the number of people who voted for him, and so on. The object no longer matters, objectivity no longer has any meaning; there remain only anger, fury, frenzy, and the infernal cycle of humiliation, resentment, and the desire for vengeance.

What we are dealing with here is an aggravated version of democratic passions. It is Trump's world, but it is also the world of those who voted for him, about 40 percent of the American electorate, not only poor Whites from the Rust Belt, urban centers hollowed out by deindustrialization, but also poor Whites from the rural parts of states such as Iowa and Wisconsin. Their anger and rage at being left behind were expressed with a force that stunned even the most experienced political observers.

To the economic and cultural reasons for this wrath must be added no doubt the most important and the most pernicious motivation: racism, in particular the desire to relegate to the garbage heap of history the eight years when America was governed by a man of color, Barack Obama.

Much has been said and written also about populism in connection with Trump's America. Populism is a poorly defined political category, often associated with both fascism and Stalinism, which is to say it may be found on the right as well as on the left. At bottom, however, it is characterized not by a particular ideology, but by a certain structure of power. Populism is clearly a degenerate form of democracy, from which it takes the idea, converted into a slogan, that power emanates from the people. This appeal to popular sovereignty is directed against social and political elites, under the guidance of a charismatic leader who both represents and exacerbates unhealthy passions.

This picture applies fairly well to Trump's America, but it fails to take into consideration an essential feature of the modern world and of the United States in particular: the aggrieved concern with victims.

During the 2016 campaign, Trump insulted whole classes of the population with a coarseness and a vulgarity that were without precedent in American political life. Remarkably, not all the members of these groups took offense; a considerable number of them found reasons to vote for him. This was notably the case with women, treated by Trump as sexual objects with whom he could do as he pleased. It was also the case—and here one may choose examples almost at random—with Mexicans, thieves and rapists all; Muslims, every last one a terrorist; liberal journalists, enemies of the American people bent on manufacturing fake news; people with motor impairments, such as the *New York Times* reporter whose limp Trump cruelly parodied on television; war heroes and former prisoners of war, such as the late Republican senator John McCain; those who died for their country, such as the young enlisted soldier of Pakistani descent whose parents found themselves the target of Trump's venomous barbs for a week; those who respect so-called taboos against the use of torture and the option of a nuclear first strike.

All these people have one thing in common. They are the sacred cows of American democracy. They are not to be criticized, on any pretext whatever—or, rather, they were not criticized until Trump came along. This sacralization of victims is best known for having given rise to the vogue of political correctness on American college campuses. But the phenomenon is much more general and comes under the head of what the cultural anthropologist Eric Gans has called "victimary resentment"[18]—the resentment of those who take it upon themselves to redress wrongs on behalf of society's victims, real or imagined. Hillary Clinton was the quintessence of this neo-Puritan self-righteousness, and the Democratic Party she represented was the champion of identity politics, which is to say the defense of oppressed minorities. Trump's stroke of malign genius—as a billionaire, a model of corruption and dishonesty—was to find a way of passing himself off as the representative of the true people, people who refused to have anything to do with homosexuals or factual truth, who found themselves at the mercy of the globalization promoted by the elites. The boorishness of their hero was wondrous to behold. Finally—finally!—someone had dared to say out loud, and with no regard for propriety, what real Americans believe.

Whatever the future holds for American democracy, the degeneracy Trump personifies may prove to be irreversible.

Misunderstandings and Confusions

Rage, much more than fear, is the enemy of clear thinking. In the matter of nuclear war, as in all other domains, Trump's reactions were governed by the destructive passions that constantly assail him. These reactions were nonetheless very instructive, no less than the equally harsh responses of his critics, for they threw into stark relief the obstacles that stand in the way of a clear understanding of the basic concepts of nuclear strategy, whether with regard to deterrence or war. It is true that these concepts are exceedingly difficult to grasp. Why bother, then, trying to elucidate them? After all, does not history since 1945 show that atomic weapons regulate themselves, that their very power makes them self-neutralizing? Donald Trump was quite right almost thirty years ago to call this feeble line of reasoning "bullshit."[19] Here we find a first reason why the questions I am concerned with in this book are of interest to so few people.

Trump is like a nine-year-old boy. As president, when his hand rested on the nuclear button, he had a fearsome toy at his disposal, the most powerful arsenal in the world. Why on earth did he not make use of it when "Little Rocket Man" defied him, this loony Communist who threatened to reduce one or two American cities to radioactive ashes? Trump, in one fell swoop, could have wiped North Korea off the face of the earth. He did not understand that, in principle, the atomic bomb serves only one purpose: preventing others from using it. But who has understood this? One would have to have a twisted mind to comprehend such a thing. Being a child can sometimes be an advantage: one is surprised at what grown-ups assume goes without saying.

The extreme violence of the words exchanged in the summer of 2017 was alarming. Trump threatened to totally destroy North Korea; Kim called Trump a "frightened dog" and a "mentally deranged dotard." In retrospect these insults border on the ridiculous, mere expressions of impotent rage having no strategic value. If they were frightening at the time, it is because people had forgotten that the very essence of deterrence is to replace the violence of weapons with that of words. "Our submarines are capable of killing fifty million people in a half-hour," a French military strategist declared in 1986. "We think that suffices to deter any adversary whatsoever."[20] That was a much more elegant way of stating the matter! The usual Gallic (and Gaullist) gambit was to threaten an adversary with "incommensurable damage." In itself, an escalation of words may be inoffensive even when it is unrestrained, because it is futile[21]— unless it is accompanied by an escalation of weapons, which is to say an arms race. The worst outcome, as we will see, comes about when weapons, simply by virtue of their existence, replace words and create a new language.

Some commentators have seen Trump as a latter-day Nixon. Frustrated by the course of the Vietnam War, Nixon had the idea of pretending to be irrational and dangerously volatile, so much so that the North Vietnamese, fearing that he was capable of doing something crazy, would sue for peace at once. The view that Trump was applying Nixon's so-called Madman Theory in the case of North Korea is yet another sign of the general incomprehension that surrounds the subject of nuclear deterrence. Far from being Nixon's invention, the Madman Theory is an integral part of deterrence. The paradox that lies at the heart of deterrence is that it is rational only insofar as it consists in making a threat that, were it actually to be carried out, would be the height of irrationality. When Nixon was informed in January 1969 that the only option available to him, in retaliating against a Soviet attack, would cause the death of at least eighty million Russians in a few hours, given the prodigious destructive power of the hydrogen bomb, he was horrified. Henry Kissinger, his national security advisor, later wondered incredulously how one could "rationally . . . make a decision to kill eighty million people."[22] Kissinger was not concerned with ethics; he was concerned with rationality—it went without saying that monstrous acts on this scale cannot be morally justified. What Kissinger rejected was the idea that killing millions could be defended on rational grounds. But what he considered to be the height of irrationality is in fact an essential element of the rationality of deterrence. It is quite wrong to suppose, as is generally done, that deterrence is effective, and indeed conceivable, only if those who do the deterring and those who are to be deterred are rational. This is usually taken to be a necessary condition that was no longer satisfied in the era of Trump and Kim and, before them, of Muammar Qaddafi, Saddam Hussein, and Mamoud Ahmadinejad. Nothing could be more untrue, however. From the moment of its conception, nuclear deterrence implied madness, whether real or imagined—though one may wonder whether the distinction still has any meaning in the atomic age. I will come back to this point in some detail in what follows.

One further remark regarding the comparison between Nixon and Trump. In order to make deterrence work, one must be able to play two roles at once: the rational strategist and the deranged statesman. This requires the talent of a very fine actor, who has the ability to be himself and at the same time the character he is portraying.[23] Nixon had this talent;[24] whether Trump does may be doubted. For Trump—and it is here that the sickness that eats away at him assumes its full importance—is at every moment a monument to his own passions. To be sure, the passions are constantly changing; but he seems to be incapable of the slightest detachment with regard to himself, incapable of examining his own life, incapable of Irony In the Socratic sense, and therefore ignorant of everything that acting on the international stage requires. This is what made him eminently dangerous when he was president. Whether the danger he represented will be uncontrollable when it runs up against Putin's own folly in Ukraine remains to be seen.

The Unreality of Large Numbers

Daniel Ellsberg is well known as a whistleblower for having copied and transmitted, first to the *New York Times* and then to the *Washington Post*, the famous Watergate Papers, whose publication hastened Nixon's fall and resignation. It was much less well known, until the appearance of his recent book, that in 1961, while working at the RAND Corporation as an economist specializing in decision theory, he was transferred to the White House and later the Pentagon where, as a member of Robert McNamara's staff, he assisted with nuclear war planning. In 1970, on leaving RAND, he copied all the documents in his safe, not only those concerning the Vietnam War but also those bearing upon nuclear war. He hesitated over which ones to publish first. It seemed to him obvious that publicizing the dangers American nuclear strategy posed not only for the United States but for the world as a whole—nothing less than an apocalyptic event leading, if not to the extinction of life on earth, then at least to the disappearance of what we call civilization—was far more important than exposing the scandalous circumstances surrounding the conduct of the Vietnam War. And yet he made the opposite choice. Ellsberg has given pragmatic reasons for doing so, such as the urgency of putting an end to an absurd conflict, but it is plain from what he says elsewhere that there was a deeper motivation: the sense of futility one is bound to feel as a prophet of nuclear doom in a world determined to remain "blind in the face of the apocalypse," to recall a phrase due to the German philosopher Günther Anders.[25]

The copied documents concerning nuclear war were set aside, then lost and never recovered. Almost a half century later, many of the originals having been declassified in the meantime and studied in considerable detail, Ellsberg decided to recount his own involvement in the decision-making of the period and to reflect upon questions that are even more topical and urgent now than they were fifty years ago. His memoir *The Doomsday Machine: Confessions of a Nuclear-War Planner* is a mine of information and analysis that cannot fail to make a profound impression on anyone who takes an interest in these questions. "Anyone" in this case should be everyone who is presently alive.

At the very outset Ellsberg recalls his shock at learning the number of deaths that the plans he had helped devise would entail on a planetary scale: six hundred million—the equivalent, as he takes care to point out, of "a hundred Holocausts."[26] Numbers on this order are so huge that they no longer have the power to terrify. Fear is a human sentiment, a noble and necessary one. But here we find ourselves outside the human condition. No greater escalation to extremes can be imagined.

The remarkable thing about horror of this magnitude is that it seems to have no limit. "People fleeing suffocation in the shelters took to the streets to escape," Ellsberg writes, "and became blazing torches unable to move in the melting asphalt. Tokyo, like Venice, was covered with canals, to which mothers raced with their children to get away from the heat. The smaller canals began to boil, and families boiled to death by the thousands."[27] He is referring here to Japan. But not to Hiroshima. He is referring to the firebombing of Tokyo on the night of 9–10 March 1945, five months before the first atomic bomb was dropped. The number of deaths was roughly the same, about 100,000. In the case of Tokyo, it took an entire night to achieve this result; in the case of Hiroshima, only half an hour. The efficiency of the operation was dramatically greater in the latter case as well: a single bomb instead of the payloads carried by three hundred bombers. In the view of General Curtis LeMay, later the head of the Strategic Air Command, who presided over the destruction of Hiroshima and Nagasaki, this was the great merit of the atomic bomb by comparison with incendiary bombs. Ellsberg was anticipated by the historians Gar Alperovitz[28] and Barton Bernstein[29] in emphasizing that no moral considerations intervened in President Truman's decision to resort to nuclear weapons. The decision was made in Potsdam, a suburb of Berlin, in the aftermath of the successful detonation (code name Trinity) of a nuclear device on 16 July 1945 at Alamogordo, New Mexico. The threshold of moral horror had already been crossed long before.

No more than passing from incendiary bombs to an atomic weapon had done, passing from the atomic to the hydrogen bomb scarcely provoked any reaction from war planners other than what might have been expected of blinkered bureaucrats responsible for counting deaths in the millions. In 1956 Ellsberg was surprised to learn that the estimate of the number of Soviet deaths caused by an American first strike had been multiplied by ten in the course of only a year.[30] Had a high-level decision been taken, that in order to deter the Soviets from attacking first it was necessary to threaten hundreds of millions dead, not merely tens of millions? The explanation turns out to have been much simpler and more trivial. Plans of attack had not changed in the least: same strategy, same targets, and so on. In the new calculation, fission bombs had given way to fusion bombs, ten times more lethal. Arithmetic had taken the place of thought—in something like the way noted by Claude Lefort in connection with voting.

My subject in this book has no popular appeal. At bottom, the reason why nuclear war does not frighten anyone is that people find it boring. The figures are so enormous that no one can make sense of them, and the strategic thinking from which they follow is so baroque that it deadens rather than excites the imagination. Already in the 1950s Günther Anders and Hannah Arendt had called attention to the growing gap between what we are capable of doing, including what we are capable of destroying, and what we are capable of thinking about or even imagining. What Arendt called the "banality" of evil[31] and Anders its "transcendence,"[32] which comes to the same thing, have been misunderstood. The basic idea, expressed by apparently opposite metaphors, is that interiority has ceased to matter. Evil is no longer defined by the intentions that give rise to an act; there is no longer anything deeper to dig down for, Arendt says, nothing to discover—all that is left is a mere surface effect.[33] But Anders is also right to say that even if it proceeds from within us, evil appears to us as originating in an unfathomable exteriority. Neither Kim nor Trump wished the war into which they risked dragging the world, like sleepwalkers,[34] any more than Kennedy and Khrushchev did during the Cuban Missile Crisis. The tragedy is that what they wished for is of no importance.[35]

Two

MAD

THE BIRTH OF A STRUCTURE

I've become more and more deeply convinced that the human
spirit must be capable of rising above dealing with other nations and human beings by threatening their existence.

RONALD REAGAN
"Address to the Nation on Defense and National Security,"
23 March 1983

Defense or Deterrence?

Anyone who has never thought carefully about nuclear deterrence
is bound to find the facts that I set down here improbable. Yet it is
only by taking them seriously that we can have a sane understanding of our present situation.

The scene unfolds in Moscow on 3 June 2000 and the days following. Bill Clinton, who will be president of the United States of
America for only a few more months, has come to hold talks with
Vladimir Putin, who has been president of his own country for less
than a month. At this summit, which had been prepared since January by teams of negotiators from the two countries, Clinton seemed
to face an impossible task. He had to convince Putin that the American plan to construct a limited system of antimissile defense was

a good thing for both countries, and that without it the agreement negotiated under the rubric of the Strategic Arms Limitation Talks (SALT) to bring about a parallel reduction of nuclear weapons could not be implemented. The Russian position was just the reverse: yes for the reduction, but only on the condition that the United States give up its antimissile defense plan. Going ahead with it would open the way to a new arms race.

Since the dissolution of the Soviet Union in December 1991, relations between Russia and the United States were no longer hostile; indeed, the two countries had a number of common interests, not least combating terrorism. How then are we to account for such a divergence in the assessment of nuclear risk? The answer is to be sought neither in differences of political culture nor in doctrinal disagreements; it depends not on norms but on facts and the hypotheses one forms in order to explain them. What would happen if a nuclear superpower resolved to protect itself against nuclear attack by means of a shield consisting of antimissile missiles? This is a question that comes under the head of the science of human behavior, if there is such a thing.

The project that Clinton presented to Putin was a very watered-down version of the famous "Star Wars" program that Ronald Reagan had introduced in a solemn address to the American people on the evening of 23 March 1983. Formally known as the Strategic Defense Initiative (SDI), the dramatic change in nuclear doctrine that Reagan announced rested on a thoroughgoing critique of deterrence, as much on the ethical plane as on that of rationality. Ever since the advent of the nuclear age, Reagan maintained, aggression had been deterred "through the promise of offensive retaliation." Everything about this tortuous vocabulary betrays the confusions inherent in the concept of nuclear deterrence. What is called a promise here is actually a threat. As for offensive retaliation, it is actually a response to an attack that is itself offensive in nature. "Wouldn't it be better," Reagan went on, in a phrase destined to be famous, "to save lives than to avenge them?" Newly developed technologies, he assured the nation, could make this dream a reality, for it was now possible to intercept and destroy strategic[1] ballistic missiles before they reach American soil and the lands of our allies. Nuclear weapons could be rendered "impotent and obsolete."

Almost two years later, in a foreword to the report on SDI published on 28 December 1984, Reagan found still stronger words to express his conviction that antimissile defense was the indispensable condition for a reduction, and even the complete elimination, of nuclear weapons. It is worth quoting from this document at some length, in order to have a clearer idea of what the categorical rejection of deterrence amounted to:

> Originally, we relied on balanced defensive and offensive weapons to deter. But over the last twenty years, the United States has nearly abandoned efforts to develop and deploy defenses against nuclear weapons, relying instead almost exclusively on the threat of nuclear retaliation. We accepted the notion that if both we and the Soviet Union were able to retaliate with devastating power even after absorbing a first strike, stable deterrence would endure. . . . There did not seem to be any alternative. The state of the art in defensive systems did not permit an effective defensive system.
>
> Today . . . new technologies are at hand which may make possible a truly effective nonnuclear defense.
>
> For these reasons and because of the awesome destructive potential of nuclear weapons, we must seek another means of deterring war. It is both militarily and morally necessary. Certainly, there should be a better way to strengthen peace and stability, a way to move away from a future that relies so heavily on the prospect of rapid and massive nuclear retaliation and toward greater reliance on defensive systems which threaten no one. . . .
>
> Our research under the Strategic Defense Initiative complements our arms reduction efforts and helps to pave the way for creating a more stable and secure world. The research that we are undertaking is consistent with all our treaty obligations, including the 1972 Anti-Ballistic Missile Treaty. . . .
>
> In the long term, we have confidence that SDI will be a

crucial means by which both the United States and the Soviet Union can safely agree to very deep reductions, and eventually, even the elimination of ballistic missiles and the nuclear weapons they carry.[2]

Tellingly, Reagan did not fail to mention the ABM Treaty by which Nixon and Brezhnev undertook in 1972 to drastically limit reliance on technologies intended to defend against nuclear attacks launched by intercontinental ballistic missiles (ICBMs). At the time—and, to a large extent, still today—such technologies were inadequate to the task. Typically they provided for the interception of one missile by another missile, and progress in developing more sophisticated systems was systematically thwarted by the ingenuity of missile designers; one finds the like of this in computer programming, where cybercriminals manage to stay a step ahead of the latest antivirus software. The fact that an intercontinental missile can be equipped with ten nuclear warheads obliges the defender to launch ten interceptors for each attacking missile. Complicating matters further, the attacker mixes warheads with decoys, as many as forty for each missile, against which the defensive system, unable to tell decoys apart from true warheads, is powerless. When Reagan said that SDI did not violate the ABM Treaty, it might have been thought that he was indulging in a bit of black humor, alluding to the possibly irremediable ineffectiveness of defensive systems; or that he had in mind only the first stage of the program, the research phase; or else that he simply mistook what he desired for reality.

Two years later Reagan made his case in person to Mikhail Gorbachev, to no avail. The opportunity to negotiate an agreement that would have changed the course of history was squandered. Their meeting took place in Reykjavik on 11–12 October 1986. Gorbachev had come to propose a plan for eliminating nuclear arms by the year 2000, but on one condition: that Reagan abandon SDI. Reagan refused. He could not go back on the promise he had made to the American people; moreover, he emphasized once again, the research program he envisioned was perfectly compatible with any reasonable interpretation of the ABM Treaty. Gorbachev suggested a compromise, that research on the viability of antimissile defenses be confined for the next ten years to the laboratory. Reagan again refused but promised to share the results of American research with the Soviets, even technical details concerning the design of the antimissile shield itself. Gorbachev did not believe a word of it. When they were about to leave Reykjavik, their talks having ended in failure, Reagan told Gorbachev that history would remember that they had stumbled over a simple word: *laboratory*—as in "laboratory research." It was the height of foolishness, but there you are.

Naturally the differences between the two sides were much more profound, for they bear on the question that has occupied us from the beginning: in the matter of nuclear war, does the possibility of reaching an agreement on mutual disarmament necessarily depend on renouncing the defense of one's country? The documentary record available to us does not say whether Gorbachev thought to put forward two apparently sensible arguments. He could have said to Reagan, "Look, if there are no longer any bombs, why construct a shield to protect yourself against them?" Or, looking at the problem the other way around, he might have pointed out that each time one side takes additional steps to protect itself, the other side has to devise new offensive means for overcoming the latest defensive innovation, as military history abundantly shows. Trench warfare was invented to deal with the problem posed by the discrepancy between a considerable increase in firepower and the lack of progress in improving troop mobility. The solution was to give absolute priority to defense over offense—to the point of absurdity, which is to say complete immobility. From this came the carnage of the First World War. To shift the balance once more in favor of the offense, by giving fresh impetus to mobile warfare, the British invented the tank. This type of escalation is the driving force of the nuclear arms race. As early as 1967, Robert McNamara, who had stayed on as secretary of defense under Lyndon Johnson, had used similar arguments in an attempt to persuade the prime minister of the Soviet Union, Alexei Kosygin, that reducing offensive weapons depended on putting an end to the deployment of antimissile systems. To this Kosygin replied that "a defensive system which prevents attacks is not a cause of the arms race."[3] The historical irony, that at this time the two countries' positions were reversed, will be obvious: the Soviet Union endorsed antimissile defense, which it was actively seeking to develop, whereas the United States objected to it—at least in the person of McNamara, a genius of military thought—for better or, above all, for worse.[4]

We will see that neither one of the arguments that I have put into Gorbachev's mouth is defensible. Both miss what makes nuclear deterrence unique in the history of defensive systems.

When Strategy Goes Mad

When Clinton visited Putin in June 2000, both leaders were thoroughly acquainted with the historical background I have just summarized. They also knew, quite obviously, that the geopolitical situation had completely changed: since the end of the Soviet Union, formally declared on 26 December 1991, the number of nuclear warheads and strategic missiles had been significantly reduced on both sides, without this having any discernible impact on security; and in the meantime the technology of antimissile defense had improved, but not nearly enough to be effective. Above all, the two leaders had the foresight to realize that a threat—though of course it was not new—loomed over the horizon like Victor Hugo's hideous black sun, ready to devour everything: nuclear terrorism, whether state-sponsored or not. Obviously they did not know the date of the leap into the abyss, the one that truly marked the entry into the third millennium of our era: 11 September 2001.

The antimissile defense plan that Clinton presented to Putin was therefore a dramatically scaled-down version of the one envisioned by Reagan. It was simply a matter of intercepting missiles that might be—or, more likely, for there could be no doubt they were being developed,[5] that would be—launched by what America called rogue states. For the moment, the list of these states included North Korea, Iraq, Iran, and Libya. What mattered to Clinton was assuring Putin that, with regard to relations between their two countries, nothing had changed. Which meant what? That America would continue to forego protecting itself against nuclear attacks originating in Russia. It is here that incredulous readers will scratch their heads. In order to understand what happened next, the important thing is not what an antimissile shield was capable of doing, but the re-iteration of a mad promise not to place any obstacle in the way of Russian missiles.

The American draft agreement that had been drawn up in January 2000 in preparation for the summit made it clear that the system of defense the United States sought to deploy "will be incapable of threatening Russia's strategic deterrence." It emphasized further-more that even if the two nations agreed to reduce the number of nuclear warheads to some 1,500 or 2,000 on each side, Russian nu-clear forces would have nothing to fear from an American defensive shield. Let it be noted in passing that, by this line of reasoning, what was to be feared was not attack but protection against attack. The American negotiators, curiously putting themselves in the position of the Russians, stressed that if Russia launched against the United States "about a thousand warheads, together with two to three times more decoys, accompanied by other advanced defense penetration aids," they could easily overwhelm the limited American system. To forestall any chance of misunderstanding, the negotiators added that the strategic forces remaining in the wake of a reduction on this scale "give each side the certain ability to carry out an *annihi-lating* counterattack," even if Russia were to protect itself by a shield equivalent to the one that the United States contemplated.[6]

To simplify outrageously, what the Americans were saying to the Russians was this: Rest assured—even after agreeing to drasti-cally reduce our respective arsenals, the shield that we are going to construct in order to protect ourselves against attacks from rogue states and terrorist groups will be easily enough penetrated by your missiles that nothing would prevent you from wiping our country off the face of the earth if we were foolishly to decide to attack first.

This way of thinking, rather mad to begin with, had now gotten crazier still. In order to persuade the Russians to yield to their will, the American negotiators openly admitted that they were prepared to adopt a strategy that everyone knew to be extremely dangerous.

The idea behind this strategy, known in military circles as launch on warning (LOW), is simple; we have already encountered it in connection with the Hawaiian false alert. If a defensive system detects incoming enemy missiles, it immediately launches a retaliatory nuclear strike without waiting for the first wave of missiles to reach their targets. In this way a country protects itself against the risk of finding itself without a defensive capability once its own missiles have been destroyed by those of the enemy. The problem is that warning sensors are known to be very unreliable, with a high rate of false positives; this is more apt to be the case with Russian systems than others. But the Americans thought that they were offering the Russians an additional guarantee—namely, that they would not attack them first with a devastating strike even if they, the Americans, were equipped with a defensive antimissile system. This arrangement was supposed to have the virtue of convincing both sides that they would find themselves on the losing end of a nuclear exchange.[7]

What was imagined to be the basis for mutually effective deterrence came at an absurdly high price, then, as American critics were quick to point out: the Russians were reassured, but the chance that a nuclear war would be unleashed by accident was now maximized.

In June 2000, Clinton failed to convince Putin, far from it. Who could be naïve enough to believe that the Americans would try to square the circle—by equipping themselves with a shield thick enough to stop missiles having a purely notional existence and thin enough to let through Russian Topol-M ICBMs—for the purpose simply of meeting the North Korean threat? No, the shield (in its later more sophisticated versions) was meant to protect against Russian missiles. This at least is what the Russians thought. At all events, Clinton had only a few months left in office and it was with his successor—perhaps the Republican George W. Bush—that they would have to negotiate. The rest is history.

MAD Exposed

In the nuclear era, there are two ways in which to defend one-self: materially, by constructing an antimissile shield, or verbally, through words that express promises and threats, which is to say deterrence. The two approaches can be combined, and this is what the United States still tries to do today, by using the first in connection with rogue states and terrorist groups and the second in connection with Russia and, potentially, China. We will see later that the distinction between the two methods must not be exaggerated, for physical actions are signs that have their own grammar. Weapons also speak. As Thomas Hobbes put it in *Leviathan* (1651), in a famous play on words, "Covenants, without the *sword*, are but *words* and of no strength to secure a man at all."[8]

The threat of nuclear reprisal, by comparison with any other extraordinary menace, is so monstrous that if it were to be acted on, one would risk destroying not only the enemy but the rest of the world at the same time, oneself included. The Americans invited the Russians to "annihilate" them if need be; plans were devised for nuclear war that would kill hundreds of millions. There seemed to be no limit to what the two nations claimed to be ready to do. France, for its part, was determined not to be left behind. It warned that it was prepared to cause "horrible destruction,"[9] "unacceptable" and "unbearable" damage "out of proportion to what is at stake in the conflict."[10] This last qualification was a deliberate affront to one of the principles of just war, the principle of proportionality, as we will see.

In principle, one does not use a sledgehammer to crush a gnat nor a cannonball to shoot a human being, but what if these are the only means at one's disposal? The disproportion is intrinsic to the instruments of death themselves. Can it be kept within certain bounds? The futility of the notion of limited nuclear war, advocated by Robert McNamara half a century ago under the name of "graduated response" and then taken seriously once more during Trump's presidency, will soon become apparent.

Clinton went to Moscow in the hope of selling the Russians on his plan for an antimissile shield, but what his visit made alarmingly clear was the logic, at once rational and insane, of nuclear deterrence. Let us begin by giving a formal description. Two nuclear powers confront one another in a mutual state of strength and weakness: they are both vulnerable because each may die as a result of aggression by the other; both are invulnerable because neither one will die before having killed its aggressor—which they will always be able to do thanks to the capacity of each party to launch a second strike, no matter how powerful the initial attack that destroys them. Both parties threaten their adversary with devastating reprisals if it departs from the status quo. Finally, neither one takes steps to protect itself. Each nation willingly exposes its population to a holocaust. Security has now become the daughter of terror: if one of the two nations were to take such steps, the other might believe that it considered itself invulnerable and therefore would act preemptively, striking first.

A system of this kind is supposed to constitute a stable equilibrium, one that is capable of absorbing external shocks. We will see nonetheless that it may degenerate, plunging both nations into the abyss of mutual annihilation if one of them launches an attack with nuclear or simply conventional forces,[11] and if the other resolves to make good on its threat of retaliation. This amounts—to use Clausewitz's image—to an escalation to extremes and, ultimately, mutual destruction.

Bizarrely, it is this very risk that gave its name to the structure: mutual assured destruction,[12] whose acronym, MAD, altogether appropriately sums up this state of affairs. For madness is exactly what we are dealing with here—only with this difference, that madness represents the culmination of human reason when reason assumes the form of rationality. Henceforth, MAD will be the focus of our attention, as Yorick's skull was for Hamlet in a way.

The advantage of a shield consisting of antimissile missiles launched on the basis of an alert by comparison with the carrying out of a threat consisting of words is that those who have made the threat, to a much greater degree than those who have made the shield, are wracked by uncertainty and the suspicion that their bluff has been called. Indeed, these doubts may be so unsettling as to deprive the threat of all deterrent force. What head of state, having only a ravaged nation to defend, would run the risk, by means of a vengeful second strike, of putting an end to human history while committing suicide at the same time? In a world of sovereign states endowed with the minimal rationality that Hobbes granted to people living in a state of nature (which is to say the instinct for self-preservation), the nuclear threat would have no credibility whatsoever. Jonathan Schell, who devoted his life to the elimination of nuclear weapons, notwithstanding the great controversy his work aroused, cast this idea in the form of a temporal paradox that I consider in the last chapter:

> Since in nuclear-deterrence theory the whole purpose of having a retaliatory capacity is to deter a first strike, one must ask what reason would remain to launch the retaliation once the first strike had actually arrived. It seems that the logic of the deterrence strategy is dissolved by the very event—the first strike—that it is meant to prevent. Once the action begins, the whole doctrine is self-canceling. It would seem that the doctrine is based on a monumental logical mistake: one cannot credibly deter a first strike with a second strike whose raison d'être dissolves the moment the first strike arrives.[13]

In other words, nuclear deterrence works as long as it works. If it ceases to work, the properties that enable it to work are nullified. It is *causa sui*—its own cause.

It is remarkable how many people, experts and laymen alike, are not convinced by this argument. They emphasize that even if it is irrational to carry out a threat of retaliation, since that would lead in principle to mutual assured destruction, military leaders might be led to do it under the influence of passion, an integral part of human nature. Two of the most powerful passions operate in support of deterrence: fear, it goes without saying, but also the desire for vengeance. It is possible that a nation on the receiving end of a nuclear first strike would not take the risk of unleashing a globally suicidal escalation, but this is far from certain. And what if it were on the verge of collapse? When Robert McNamara learned, in 1992, about the Soviet delegation of authority to local commanders to fire nuclear missiles during the Cuban Missile Crisis thirty years earlier, he said: "No one should believe that a U.S. force could have been attacked by tactical nuclear weapons without responding with nuclear warheads. And where would it have ended? In utter disaster."[14]

Contrary to the widespread belief that, since Hiroshima, there has been a taboo among Americans against the use of atomic weapons,[15] a majority of them, yielding to the incitement of President Trump, were recently found to favor bombing North Korea[16] in the event that country launched a nuclear attack on the American island of Guam.[17] If a city in the United States were to be targeted, there can be little doubt that Kim Jong Un's country would immediately be annihilated. It might be objected that anticipation of the retrospective judgment of history would act as a brake. Would the first country, and the only one until now, to drop atomic bombs on civilian populations dare also to be the first country to do it again? Germany has not managed completely to wipe away the moral stain it brought upon itself in the middle of the twentieth century; indeed, it may never succeed in doing so. Can America today run the risk of letting the person in whom it has confided supreme power put an end to Western civilization? It ought instead to heed the wise words of Nikita Khrushchev, who took the first steps to arrest the lethal escalation of the Cuban Missile Crisis. A few months afterward, he asked: "What good would it have done me in the last hour of my life to know that though our great nation and the United States of America were in complete ruins, the national honor of the Soviet Union was intact?"[18]

The French, for their part, have a disturbing case study to contemplate in the confession of their former president Valéry Giscard d'Estaing. In his memoirs, Giscard recalls a war game conducted in the basement of Élysée Palace in May 1980 under the direction of the chief of staff of the armed forces, Guy Méry. The simulation assumed that Soviet forces, having arrived in Frankfurt, looked to press their advantage further to the west, and that allied forces were unable to mount any organized resistance; only French forces were in a position to do this. General Méry then addressed Giscard: "Monsieur le président, the Commander of the First Army requests your permission to use, if he judges it necessary, his tactical nuclear weapons." Giscard silently reflected, reasoning thus:

> I imagined how events would unfold: French units fire their short-range missiles against the Soviet armies occupying West German territory. . . . Tomorrow a Soviet nuclear strike will destroy all of our divisions, and the bases of our tactical air force, in Alsace and the East.
>
> Simultaneously, the Soviet commander will threaten us with severe reprisals in the event of another nuclear attack. Given the semi-annihilation of our forces, even before our territory has been invaded, the decision to explode a strategic warhead, thereby causing "mutual assured destruction," would amount to the last gesture of an irresponsible leader.

Then he turned to Méry and said, "Under the circumstances, I do not authorize the firing [of short-range missiles]."[19]

Most of those who recall this passage in Giscard's memoirs stop there. It seemed to be evidence of something quite extraordinary: a head of state who, faced with the spectre of mutual assured destruction, vowed that he would have refrained from pressing the nuclear button. To be sure, his avowal came after the fact, but the moment it was made, the credibility of the French nuclear force suffered a grave blow.

The next part of Giscard's account deserves no less to be remembered, however, for it seems partly to contradict this view. In the course of a second exercise, Giscard pondered once more the risk of a fatal escalation of violence:

> (And then, with regard to mutual assured destruction, whatever may happen—and I put these words between parentheses in order to emphasize that this decision has always been rooted in the depths of my being—whatever may happen I will never initiate a course of action that would lead to the annihilation of France. *If her destruction were to be brought*

about first by an adversary, I would take the necessary steps
to avenge her at once. But otherwise I wish to leave to her
countryside, to her houses, to her trees, to the water of her
ponds and rivers, to the faithfulness of her people to their
convictions, now hidden from them, the ultimate chance of
one day reviving French culture.)[20]

In the sentence I have italicized, Giscard presents the need to exact
vengeance almost as a moral and political duty—the only motive,
apart from madness, real or imagined, that can explain, if not justify, the decision to deliver oneself up to mutual assured destruction
as one might sacrifice oneself to a divinity.

Once we abandon the assumption that actors are "rational," in
the stunted sense given this word by the disciplines that instruct
technocratic elites today (neoclassical economics, rational choice
theory, strategic thought as it is narrowly conceived by game theory,
and so on), ignoring the role of the passions in human life, nuclear
deterrence can be seen to escape the curse of self-refutation. To conclude that deterrence depends only on the irrationality of actors,
however, would be worse than a mistake; it would be a crime.

To Deter or to Preempt?[21]

At this point in the early twenty-first century, then, the choice between defense and deterrence remains in principle an unresolved
question for the United States no less than Russia. It may be objected
that debate should not be limited to these two countries at a time
when new threats are slipping through the cracks that the often
mute confrontation of the superpowers has left open. It is common
today to speak of a new nuclear era characterized by proliferation
and terrorism. Daniel Ellsberg has vigorously taken issue with this
opinion. The greatest danger today for the survival of the human
race and, beyond that, of life on earth remains the prospect of a nuclear war between the two superpowers, as it was during the Cold
War: "For over fifty years, all-out thermonuclear war has been . . . a
catastrophe waiting to happen."[22]

By now Ellsberg has lost all patience with received wisdom on nuclear matters. The opposition between defense and deterrence is misleading, he holds, and conceals a grave deception with regard to the threat of a first strike:

> The basic elements of American readiness for nuclear war remain today what they were almost sixty years ago: Thousands of nuclear weapons remain on hair-trigger alert, aimed mainly at Russian military targets including command and control, many in or near cities. The *declared* official rationale for such a system has always been primarily the supposed need to deter—or if necessary respond to—an aggressive Russian nuclear first strike against the United States. That widely believed public rationale is a deliberate deception. Deterring a surprise Soviet nuclear attack—or responding to such an attack—has *never* been the only or even the primary purpose of our nuclear plans and preparations. The nature, scale, and posture of our strategic nuclear forces has always been shaped by the requirements of quite different purposes: to attempt to limit the damage to the United States from Soviet or Russian retaliation to a *U.S. first strike* against the USSR or Russia. This capability is, in particular, intended to strengthen the credibility of U.S. threats to initiate limited nuclear attacks, or escalate them—U.S. threats of "first use"—to prevail in regional, initially non-nuclear conflicts involving Soviet or Russian forces or their allies.[23]

Ellsberg concludes: "Though officially denied, preemptive 'launch on warning' (LOW)—either on tactical warning of an incoming attack or strategic warning that nuclear escalation is probably impending—has always been at the heart of our strategic alert [system]."[24]

In order to fully grasp this essential point, nothing is more helpful than to reflect upon a familiar name for preemption (that is, launching a first strike), the oxymoronic "striking second first." The same idea may be expressed in several ways: answering before being attacked; retaliating even before enemy missiles have been launched; punishing the criminal by eliminating him before he commits his crime. All these formulations describe a paradoxical sort of temporal inversion that, as we shall see, is the signature of a quite specific metaphysics. Earlier we encountered it in the case of launch on warning. Preemption magnifies the paradox.

Ellsberg defends a maximalist position. On this view, deterrence has always had a very secondary, if not actually nonexistent role in American nuclear doctrine and policy.[25] To be sure, a great many historical facts, which Ellsberg knows better than anyone, argue in its favor, at least up until the signing of the ABM Treaty in 1972—the perfect embodiment, as we have seen, of the logic of mutual assured destruction in its most paradoxical form. The fundamental assumption of MAD is that neither party attacks first. The stalemate that results from this is so peculiar that it was necessary to coin the phrase "nuclear peace"—another way of saying "cold war." It is utterly mistaken, Ellsberg says, to suppose that this curious peace is what the United States has sought from the moment it developed a nuclear capability. The primary objective was never to guarantee that it would not attack first; to the contrary, the objective was to make its adversary believe that it was in fact ready to attack first. The reversal is complete. But why then could the American determination to attack the enemy by surprise, in the form of a preemptive nuclear strike, seem in the least doubtful to the Russians? Precisely because they would still possess the ability to launch a second strike. The way to dispel such doubts was therefore to limit as far as possible the damaging effects of a retaliatory strike. As against MAD, then, it was a matter of publicizing America's resolve to protect itself.

Ellsberg claims that not a single American president since Truman has undertaken not to be the first to use nuclear weapons. Many of them were prepared to launch a preemptive strike in response to what they considered to be an imminent attack, whether conventional or nuclear. Ellsberg's thesis was corroborated in February 2018 when John Bolton, two months before becoming Trump's new national security advisor, stated that he found it perfectly legitimate that the United States should respond to what he called the imminent threat posed by North Korea by striking first, wiping it off the face of the earth. In so doing, Bolton did no more than take his place in a firmly established tradition. More than a decade earlier, George W. Bush and his partner Dick Cheney had thought of a more expeditious alternative to negotiations with Iran in order to prevent it from equipping itself with atomic weapons: destroying it by means of a preemptive attack. The use here, by the way, of the word *preemptive* is abusive since Iran was not a nuclear power at the time.

If Ellsberg is right, then, there has never been a taboo against the use of nuclear weapons. The atomic bomb is in no way thought of as something not to be used, as the theory of deterrence would have it; it is a weapon ready to hand if an enemy threatens you or tries otherwise to impose its will. In the long-standing debate on preemption versus deterrence, Ellsberg says, preemption has always carried the day, and there is no reason to think that it will not continue to do so in the future. The world is therefore a much more dangerous place than we imagine, falsely reassured as we are by the supposedly self-refuting character of the nuclear threat. Ellsberg is nonetheless obliged to recognize that, since 1945, neither side has done anything more than threaten to carry out a first strike.[26] He does not take seriously the possibility that deterrence might in fact have counted for something in this connection. Here we run up against the limits of his argument.

Before examining the "doomsday machine" that gives Ellsberg's book its title, it will be useful to make a detour through the Cuban Missile Crisis, in which he played an important role. With narrative skill worthy of Tom Clancy, Ellsberg conveys the suspense surrounding the clash of wills between Kennedy and Khrushchev, where what was at stake was nothing less than the survival of humanity. Both men were conscious of this; neither one desired war. And yet each threatened the other with extinction in order to obtain a better deal: the withdrawal of American missiles from Turkey in exchange for the removal of Soviet missiles from Cuba. For this they were prepared to delay for a few hours the moment when agreement had to be reached, even if that meant increasing the risk that both would be plunged into the abyss—a risk that some of their advisors had already reckoned to be 10 percent. As an expert in game theory, Ellsberg well knew (though he says nothing of it in his book) that what was at issue here was a zero-sum game (what one side wins, the other loses) for small stakes at the edge of the abyss. This is the structure of MAD.[27]

One of the most extraordinary apocalypses that did not occur, to recall the expression I used earlier, is well known today, even if it took forty years to discover all its details, including the name of its hero, Second Captain Vasily Alexandrovich Arkhipov. Readers born before 1962 would almost surely no longer be alive if Arkhipov had not acted as he did that day; younger readers no doubt would never have been born.

On Saturday, 27 October 1962, a Soviet submarine cruising in the Saragasso Sea, northeast of Cuba, was spotted and encircled by the American aircraft carrier USS *Randolph* and an escort of eleven destroyers. *B-59* was commanded by Captain Valentin Grigorievich Savitsky, one of three officers on board along with Arkhipov and a political officer, Ivan Semonovich Maslennikov. The American vessels had begun to send the signal agreed upon with the Soviet general staff for the purpose of ordering an enemy submarine to resurface. But Savitsky had not been informed of this procedure. The signal took the form of exploding depth charges near the hull of *B-59*; the captain thought that he was actually being attacked by the Americans—the first in a series of increasingly grave misunderstandings, false alerts, and failures of communication. Conditions inside the submarine were hellish. The temperature had reached between fifty and sixty degrees Celsius (122–140 degrees Fahrenheit), and the members of the crew were dropping like flies. On top of all of this, communications with headquarters in Moscow were cut off.

Savitsky did not even know whether war had begun. Exhausted, at the end of his tether, he was about to issue the order to launch a nuclear torpedo. That Soviet submarines in Cuban waters were carrying atomic bombs was unknown to the Americans—and was to remain unknown to them until 2002. Collecting his wits, Savitsky remembered that he had to obtain the authorization of his political officer in order to take so fatal a decision. Maslennikov gave his approval.

It was the will of chance or Providence that Arkhipov should have been on board *B-59* that day. Although they held the same rank, Arkhipov was under Savitsky's orders. But Arkhipov was also the chief of staff of the entire flotilla of F-class submarines sent to Cuba. Below Savitsky at the level of this particular submarine, he was above him at a higher level: in formal logic, this rather rare configuration is known as a tangled hierarchy.[28] Savitsky therefore believed that he needed to have Arkhipov's approval as well. Arkhipov withheld it, however, on the ground that Moscow had not given its authorization. The order to fire was therefore not issued and the submarine surfaced.

Recounting this story,[29] Ellsberg does what all of us do on hearing the tale of an apocalypse that came within a hair's breadth of becoming a reality: we wonder what would have happened if . . . . A sequence of counterfactual propositions[30] immediately springs to mind. If Arkhipov had been on a submarine other than *B-59*, it is highly probable that Savitsky would have given the order to fire. The USS *Randolph* and its destroyer escort would have been swallowed up in a terrifying nuclear explosion. The American military command, believing that the Soviet submarines carried no atomic weapons, would have inferred that the attack came from Cuba. Five days earlier, on 22 October, President Kennedy had made it known that if such a thing were to occur, the United States would launch a total nuclear attack on the Soviet Union. It is easy to imagine the rest. In the real world, the crisis was peacefully resolved the following day, 28 October.

Each of the links in this chain of inference refers to a contingent event or state of affairs, one that might have not happened or that might have been different. The weakest link, the most shocking aspect of this account, is that the American command did not know that the Soviet submarines were equipped with nuclear torpedoes. U.S. intelligence was faulty, to be sure. But this is beside the point: the stunning thing is that the Soviets had not informed the Americans of the situation beforehand. If an atomic weapon were really a means of deterrence, a nation possessing one could be expected at a minimum to let the enemy know that it had such a weapon and that it was prepared to use it. In that case the USS *Randolph* would no doubt have been more prudent in approaching the Soviet submarine.

The neglect to communicate so vital a piece of information immediately puts one in mind of the concept of a "doomsday machine," which figures in Stanley Kubrick's 1964 film *Dr. Strangelove*. Kubrick borrowed it from Ellsberg's RAND colleague, the physicist Herman Kahn, author of a widely read book of the period, *On Thermonuclear War*.[31] The idea is simple, at least on paper. The surest way to lend credibility to the threat of devastating reprisals on which deterrence is based is to make its execution automatic. This disposes of the ethical and strategic dilemmas that tormented statesmen from Kennedy to Giscard d'Estaing. In a certain sense, the nation that fires first is responsible for the holocaust that follows since the response is inhuman. In Kubrick's film, the Soviets had invented a machine that would immediately destroy all life on earth in response to an American first strike. The problem is that, when the story begins, they had not informed the Americans of its existence. A fanatic brigadier general, acting on his own authority, then orders a B-52 armed with hydrogen bombs to drop its payload on a target in Siberia: once on its way, the plane cannot be called back. Far from being a parody, Kubrick's film is actually a documentary, as Martin Hellman once quipped. Ellsberg wholly shares this opinion.[32]

The question of delegation is revelatory in this regard. Citizens of countries that are both democracies and nuclear powers, as in the case of France and the United States, find it reassuring that the final decision about whether to press the nuclear button is reserved exclusively for the chief of state, acting in consultation with military chiefs of staff and the secretary of defense. One of the most symbolic moments in the transfer of power between an outgoing president and his successor is the handover of the nuclear launch codes. It is supposed to be a mark of civilization that the monopoly on ultimate violence rests in the hands of the man or woman who embodies the nation. A moment's reflection will suffice, however, to show not only that this idea is implausible but that it verges on nonsense—and pernicious nonsense at that. For if it were true under all circumstances that a single person, always the same one, had the right to order a nuclear attack, deterrence would be completely impossible. A nation on the verge of launching a first strike would have only to begin by taking out the enemy's head of state ("decapitation," in the jargon of nuclear planners) in order to paralyze any inclination to retaliate. Deterrence enjoys credibility only if it has the form of a hydra with a thousand heads, each of which regenerates itself in several copies once it is cut off. This is indeed the case in France and the United States, unbeknownst to their own citizens. This is what is called delegation—the delegation of the authority to unleash a nuclear war capable of putting an end to civilization.

In the American case, at least, thanks again to Daniel Ellsberg, we know that delegation, like a cancer or a fractal structure,[33] has an almost irresistible power of replication. The same reasons that oblige a head of state to delegate his or her authority to a handful of generals and admirals apply to each of them in turn. Complicating matters still further, technical, meteorological, and military obstacles—all those things that make up what Clausewitz called the "fog of war"—are liable every day at any moment to interrupt communication between the person who delegates authority and those to whom authority is delegated. Whence the downward branching of delegation to ever lower and unexpected levels.

Of all this, the public is quite unaware. It is believed that the chief executive, who is also the commander-in-chief of the armed forces, has supreme power. In France, the paramount need for military secrecy is always cited, and nothing more is said of it. Thus Bruno Tertrais, the deputy director of the Foundation for Strategic Research, maintains that in France, as in the United States, "the system is designed so that the president can engage nuclear forces without opposition." He insists, without fear of contradiction, on the decisive role of "governmental supervision" in authenticating the command for missiles to be fired, in seeing to it that "it is indeed the legitimate authority—the president—who gives the order" and that "only the presidential order is executed." No reference is made to delegation of any kind.[34] There is every reason to believe that this comforting fable of unilateral executive authority is a sinister deception. France needs the equivalent of an Ellsberg.[35]

But why hide the truth from the people? The answer is obvious: if delegation is necessary to make deterrence work, it is also very dangerous because it considerably increases the chance that the decision to fire might be made owing to an impulsive act or by accident. As is often the case, not only with regard to nuclear warfare but also to the use of nuclear power in the civilian sector,[36] it is fear on the part of those who govern of the fear that the governed might well be expected to feel if the truth were told that explains the lack of official transparency and the resort to lying. Governments tremble before their own people.

By contrast, nothing explains—and still less justifies—nuclear powers hiding their practice of delegation *from their enemies*. Nevertheless that was invariably the case during the Cold War, beginning with the United States. The Soviet Union did not long delay in following its example, as we have seen in connection with the Cuban Missile Crisis, since the Americans were unaware not only that the enemy submarines were equipped with nuclear torpedoes but also that their commanders had been delegated authority to launch an attack in the event that communications with Moscow were cut off. In the last analysis, the deterrent effect of delegation exists only to the extent that the enemy is aware of its existence. Did it take Kubrick's film to make this understood? The incredible blunder of keeping delegation secret Ellsberg calls the "Strangelove Paradox."[37] To put it another way, not to reveal the existence of a delegation mechanism is to invite an enemy who feels threatened to launch a preemptive first strike in the hope of being able to decapitate its adversary. If it discovers too late that there is not one head but a hydra with multiple heads, the harm is done and nuclear catastrophe awaits.

Ellsberg suggests that it is the fear of frightening one's own people, one's allies, and the world as a whole that explains this strange and counterproductive silence with regard to the enemy, a sort of contagion of secrecy.[38] Whether or not he is right, it seems clear that deterrence has indeed been the poor relation of nuclear geopolitics for almost seventy years now.

The Difficult Birth of MAD

And what if Ellsberg's suggestion masks a more profound truth? After all, when he writes that "the [American] hope of successfully avoiding mutual annihilation by a decapitating attack has always been as ill-founded as any other,"[39] it is MAD that he has in mind. Now, as we have seen, MAD paradoxically conceives of deterrence in terms of its failure. Ellsberg finds it incomprehensible that the practice of delegation should have gone unacknowledged during the Cold War—a nuclear war that did not happen—for in that case, deterrence itself is doomed to failure, sooner or later, by an absurd silence. It is nonetheless fortunate that deterrence, even when it is absent, remains present in another way, not as doctrine, but as a *negative* point of reference, concentrating our attention on that which absolutely must be avoided: a war that no one can win and that will destroy everyone. Preemption, by contrast, aims at avoiding war by annihilating the adversary with a first strike.

That MAD was brought into the world only with the greatest difficulty is amply demonstrated by the nuclear arms race between the two superpowers that lasted until the signing of the first arms limitation agreement in 1991.[40]

In 2018, Trump boasted of having a larger organ than Kim, the sort of thing children say in schoolyards, backing up words with actions.[41] In 1961, American leaders were panicked at the thought of having fewer strategic nuclear weapons than the Soviets, when in fact they had ten times more.[42] In each case the logic of MAD had not even crossed the minds of the protagonists. To be sure, great-power status carried with it the illusory impression of omnipotence conferred by possession of atomic weapons, as Günther Anders was perhaps the first to point out, sixty-five years ago.[43] Today, countries such as Iran and North Korea are persuaded of its truth; France, for its part, continues to maintain that it "deserves" its permanent seat

on the United Nations Security Council on account of its nuclear capability.[44] In principle, however, the size of the organ is not important. If you can already destroy the earth a hundred times over, what
is the point of trying to do more than that? Deterrence is the great
equalizer. The weakest power can still cause irreparable damage to
the strongest—as Hobbes long ago demonstrated in his fictive por-
trait of the state of nature. This is the basis of French doctrine, summarized by the phrase "Deterrence of the strong by the weak."

If MAD had worked as it was supposed to, the world would never
have witnessed the insane arms race that led to the United States
having more than 30,000 nuclear warheads in 1966 and the Soviet
Union more than 40,000 in 1986. Trump's ignorance had glorious
antecedents.

The spirit of MAD has long been foreign to the Soviet Union as
well. David Holloway, in a remarkable study on the history of Soviet
strategic thought between 1955 and 1972,[45] notes that after Stalin's
death the major fear of military planners was not being able to respond to a surprise nuclear attack by American forces. Their ap-
prehensions were justified, as it turns out, for American strategists
were sorely tempted to be finished with the Soviet menace once and
for all by means of an unanswerable first nuclear strike. The Soviets modified their planning accordingly, with a view not only to
constructing an antiballistic missile shield at once, but also, like the
Americans, to equipping themselves with a preemptive first-strike
capability. Yet Khrushchev was under no illusion about the possibility of annihilating an adversary who would still have the capacity
of retaliating. The force of circumstance therefore drew him nearer
to the spirit of MAD.

In the late 1950s, in the United States, a few academic experts
took issue with the dominant opinion among military strategists,
asserting the advantages of deterrence over preemption. The most
persuasive voice was that of Bernard Brodie, nicknamed the "American Clausewitz." Brodie was the first great theoretician of MAD;
French doctrine, with which he was quite familiar, may have helped
shaped his thinking. His influential book *Strategy in the Missile Age*
(1959) is remembered not least for these famous lines: "Thus far the

chief purpose of our military establishment has been to win wars. From now on its chief purpose must be to avert them."[46] If atomic weapons were to be useful, this could not be through their deployment but through the threat of their deployment. Brodie added: "A plan and policy which offer a good promise of deterring war . . . is by orders of magnitude better in every way than one which depreciates the objective of deterrence in order to improve somewhat the chances of winning."[47]

The Soviets were not prepared just then to listen to this point of view. Things changed after Khrushchev's ouster in October 1964, Holloway says, in part owing to the influence of the analytical tools that Robert McNamara introduced into American policy making, many of which had been invented and developed at the RAND Corporation: operations research, systems theory, rational choice theory, and game theory. With the backing of the prime minister, Alexei Kosygin, emphasis was placed on antimissile defense. It soon became apparent, however, at about the same time on both sides of the Pacific, that the requisite technology had not been perfected and perhaps never would be. No antimissile shield that occasionally fails could be relied on. If only one missile gets through, it will be one too many.

By the late 1960s, Holloway concludes, both superpowers had adopted a MAD-type strategy. But it was not pure. The key concepts, in addition to mutual assured destruction, were damage limitation and partial destruction of enemy retaliatory capabilities. Pure MAD assumed, to the contrary, that neither side takes steps to protect itself, each side acknowledging that the other, owing to its second-strike capability, has the capacity to launch a devastating counterattack that will annihilate the aggressor. This was the gist of Clinton's message to Putin in Moscow in June 2000. The triumph of MAD had nonetheless occurred almost thirty years earlier with the signing of the ABM Treaty by Nixon and Brezhnev, also in Moscow, on 26 May 1972.

The abandonment of preemption for deterrence and the renunciation of defense in favor of deterrence both proceeded from the same conclusion—namely, that the violence of nuclear weapons is so extreme that there is no possible protection against them, whether the attack takes the form of a first strike by the enemy or of the enemy's response to one's own first strike. There was no guarantee, however, that the triumph of MAD would not turn out to be a Pyrrhic victory.

Three

The Pure Theory of MAD

There is no limit to the extent of error, or of horror, to which logic may lead when it is applied to matters not pertaining to pure intelligence.

HENRI BERGSON
The Two Sources of Morality and Religion

Thinking the Unthinkable

The existence of nuclear weapons poses an extreme challenge to our powers of understanding. With their invention, there suddenly emerged in human history an unprecedented possibility: the self-destruction of humanity itself—an event that, if it were to occur, would not only deprive history of all meaning but also cause it never to have had any, since there would be no one left to remember it.

This absolute nothingness is unimaginable. It is a sort of black hole that swallows up all our attempts to make sense of nuclear warfare. Hence the extreme abstraction of these efforts, which assign an essential role to options that nonetheless are presumed never to be chosen because it is inconceivable that they might be chosen and to counterfactual universes that are presumed to be impossible. The foundations of both rational choice theory and of ethics are therefore fatally undermined. Only metaphysics, to some extent at least, can provide a stable ground for analysis.

With a few notable exceptions, French philosophers have taken little interest in the properly metaphysical dimension of nuclear weapons, conceived not as a guarantee of peace but as instruments of death, which obviously they are. That this can sometimes be forgotten passes all understanding. Let us turn instead to the analytic metaphysics developed by David K. Lewis, sometimes called the Leibniz of the twentieth century for having revisited the theory of possible worlds, and also the versions due to Gregory Kavka and David Gauthier, among others, as well as the post-Heideggerian perspective elaborated by Günther Anders, one of the greatest European thinkers in this domain, and the anthropology of violence and the sacred pioneered by René Girard. All these schools of thought, rooted to one degree or another in antinomic traditions, have grown up in the shadow of the atomic threat. Quite remarkably, they are all in agreement with regard to the essential points at issue.

The format I have adopted in this chapter and the next one is very different from the style of the first two chapters.[1] My purpose so far has been to introduce and discuss a number of fundamental concepts, illustrating them by reference to a series of emblematic moments in the nuclear history of the world since 1945. Naturally these examples are in no way exhaustive, nor do they even constitute a basic chronology of the period. While the method I have adopted makes certain ideas and modes of reasoning easier to grasp, it has the great disadvantage of situating them in a historical context that has the singular property, no doubt owing to an exceptional streak of luck, of having avoided the very fate with which this book is concerned: nuclear war and the abomination of desolation that would have resulted from it. Had it occurred, neither the author nor the readers of this book would be present to speak of it—thus the central paradox of my inquiry. It is therefore necessary to speak of something that can be spoken of only if it does not exist. In reading the tens of thousands of pages that have been written on the subject—and my own do not escape this criticism—one often has the impression that the subject itself is hidden. To speak of it, we are obliged to join the mad hero of Joseph Conrad's *Heart of Darkness* in crying out, "The horror! The horror!"—words that point to something abominable without saying what it is.[2]

1. The Logical Structure of Mutual Assured Destruction

1.1 The MAD structure has become a fundamental element of human history. Even when it seems to be forgotten or absent, the mere possibility of its return produces quite real effects. There can be no doubt that this possibility will not cease to be actualized until some unknown time in the future. We must be forever vigilant.

The MAD structure is an ideal object of study for a whole range of theoretical disciplines, from metaphysics, moral philosophy, and ethics to game theory and rational choice theory. In a few particularly interesting cases, analysis of the logic of nuclear deterrence has opened up new directions in research and indeed brought about a renaissance of some of these disciplines.[3]

Not the least of the fascinating aspects of MAD is that it has cast new light on some of the oldest problems of philosophy—as if human beings, confronted with the unbearable prospect of their own disappearance, came at last to doubt what for more than twenty-five hundred years has been taken to constitute a sound basis for rational thought.

1.2 The predicate *nuclear*, inasmuch as it refers to a particular technique of destruction, is not what gives MAD its distinctive features. These features are peculiar to a situation where two nations are capable of annihilating each other as organized societies. For the first time in human history, owing to their immense destructive power, nuclear weapons have embodied this structure. "Human violence at the international level," Steven P. Lee observes, "has now become like human violence at the individual level, in that societies can now destroy each other as readily as individuals have always been able to do."[4] The destruction of a society, which is something much more than the ruin and subjection of its institutions of government, nonetheless does not require the murder of all the human beings of which it is composed. As in the case of an individual person, there is a quantitative threshold beyond which the accumulation of blows and wounds causes death. History does, of course, record cases where a society or a culture disappeared in the aftermath of a military defeat. But this outcome did not come about during the course of a war, nor was *mutual* annihilation possible in the past. The reciprocity of total destruction is the most important feature of the MAD structure.

The essential difference between the nuclear threat and all previous military threats is that the threat is no longer a matter of material or political advantage, reckoned in terms of territory or domination. Strictly speaking, there is nothing that the two adversaries, at the moment of their confrontation, are determined to fight over. The threat bears upon the very existence of each party. It is a threat of extinction. This situation came into being for the first time in the 1960s. It is no less urgent now than it was then.

1.3 My purpose in this chapter and the one following is to examine the grammar of the arguments that have been advanced in order to approve or condemn the MAD structure on prudential as well as ethical grounds. Prudential norms bear upon the effectiveness of military actions with regard to their objective, which is to assure the security of a nation. In this chapter I am concerned solely with actions that may properly be characterized as defensive—that is, actions that are taken in order to protect the legitimate sovereignty of a nation that finds itself under attack by a foreign power. The ethical norms that concern us here are of two types. The first involves defensive norms that come under the head of the just war tradition. Since nuclear deterrence manifestly cannot be accounted for in terms of this tradition, whose foundations it completely subverts, we will have to broaden our inquiry to include norms falling under a second category: common morality, which is itself plural.

One may wonder what relevance ethical considerations have in connection with nuclear war, above all in a country such as France, where the state has taken upon itself responsibility for deciding one of the most fundamental questions for the life of the nation and where democratic institutions serve as an excuse for the absence of moral reflection. The ritual of voting can never replace rational debate, however. Even those who claim that efficiency matters above all in an institution such as national defense cannot ignore the possibility that it may come to violate its own norms or even common morality, for in that case the institution would be in crisis and its efficiency would be gravely impaired as a result. Realists are pleased to point out that when ethics is not compatible with the national interest, it is ethics that is thrown by the wayside, but that is not the end of the matter. The fact remains that the norms of just war have always played an important role in conferring legitimacy on the military. Politically, they have made it possible to stake out a position intermediate between realism and pacifism. What these norms stipulate is not, or not usually, sharply at variance with the requirements of prudence. It is contrary to morality to attack civilians, but until the invention of atomic weapons, attacking civilians seldom yielded a decisive military advantage. Defensive war was justified morally by the same arguments that were used at the individual level to justify the principle of legitimate self-defense.

Here let us introduce the principle of tolerable divergence. It is satisfied when what is required by ethical norms differs only marginally from what is required by the norms of prudence. It is this principle, as we will see, that is undermined by nuclear deterrence. The just war tradition then finds itself thrown back on the side of pacifism, with the result that it becomes politically irrelevant since it can no longer provide a legitimate basis for the use of armed force. That ought to be enough to unsettle the most obstinate realist with regard to defense. But there is another reason, a more important one from our point of view, that makes the ethical issue unavoidable—namely, that the study of the prudential aspects of nuclear deterrence is logically inseparable from the analysis of deterrence in ethical terms.

The arguments advanced in this debate have a branching structure. Descending along the branches, at the nodes, one encounters increasingly fine conceptual distinctions. The consensus that prevails at the level of the main trunk tends to unravel once one reaches the lowest branches.

2. Received Opinion and the Moral Paradox

2.1 A nuclear conflict is unjustifiable from either a prudential or an ethical standpoint. This dual conclusion commands universal or nearly universal assent.

2.1.1 In prudential terms, as a general proposition, a nation is all the more likely to make war as it anticipates that its gains will be greater than its losses. The magnitude of these gains and losses depends in large part on whether the nation in question emerges victorious from the war. A nuclear war renders these notions obsolete; indeed, strictly speaking, the very word *war* no longer applies. Nevertheless, for the sake of convenience, I will continue to use it. Neither adversary can expect a net positive benefit, and the damage caused to each of them cannot help but be unacceptable.

Can a nuclear war be limited? Possibly, but only if both adversaries practice moderation. Cooperation is required if mutual moderation is to be achieved, yet there is practically no chance of this occurring. The confusion that characterizes all military activity in times of war (what Clausewitz called "friction") and the absence of supervision that accompanies it almost unavoidably have the consequence, owing to the extreme power of atomic weapons, of causing not less damage, as in the case of conventional wars, but more damage.

These conclusions do not depend on the manner in which a nation enters into conflict. Even if it does no more than respond to a limited nuclear attack, there is only a tiny chance that this response will not provoke an escalation leading to its total destruction. From a prudential point of view, and no matter how one approaches the problem, it is universally agreed that entering into a nuclear conflict is a fatal error.

2.1.2 With regard to the ethical norms laid down by the doctrine of just war, which is to say the principles of proportionality and discrimination, entering into a nuclear conflict is equally unjustified.

The principle of proportionality stipulates that, taking into account all the parties concerned, a war must produce more good than harm. A nuclear conflict evidently violates this principle to an even greater degree than it does the norms of prudence, since the harm caused to one adversary is added to the harm caused to the other.

The principle of discrimination prohibits violence against innocents—that is, citizens of the opposing nation who are not involved in the war effort. A nuclear conflict, whose extremely probable outcome is the annihilation of the adversary's society (as well as one's own), is bound to transgress this second principle.

Defensive war, in its conventional form, is generally considered to be justified on both prudential and ethical grounds. With the introduction of nuclear weapons, this situation is radically altered. The principle of tolerable divergence continues to be satisfied, however, since morality and prudence find themselves in agreement.

2.2 Nevertheless, we are not concerned here with the question of whether a nation should enter into a nuclear conflict. We want to know how to avoid such a conflict. Until recently, avoiding war has constituted a secondary objective, subordinate to the imperatives of national defense. Under the regime of mutual assured destruction, however, it has become the primary objective. Avoiding war is precisely the objective of deterrence.

Let us begin by considering received opinion in this matter. The orthodox view is that nuclear deterrence is justified in respect of prudence, but not of ethics.

2.2.1 With regard to prudential considerations, great emphasis is placed on the remarkable effectiveness of deterrence historically. The Cold War did not degenerate into open conflict, it is often pointed out—as if deterrence were responsible for this state of affairs, and the many apocalypses that did not occur can simply be ignored.

Let us distinguish between the capacity to counteract and the capacity to punish. The former, which bears upon the gains that an adversary hopes to obtain by means of war, is the essence of deterrent force in its classic form: the ability to prevent an adversary from achieving the military objectives it has set for itself. The ability to punish, which involves the damage that can be inflicted upon an adversary's society, bears upon the losses that the adversary expects to incur. In terms of deterrence, the capacity to punish is much more effective than the capacity to counteract. The threat of a society's total annihilation has a far more paralyzing effect than fear of military defeat. Under the reign of MAD, war is not capable of protecting a nation; only deterrence can do this. As Robert Jervis put it, "Coercion, not brute force, *deterrence, not defense,* are the function of our weapons."[5]

2.2.2 The orthodox view is much less assured with regard to the ethical dimension of the problem. We have already noted Reagan's doubts, echoed at the time by the American bishops, about the possibility of morally justifying nuclear deterrence.

The doctrine of just war fully confirms these doubts. It upholds the same principle with regard to deterrence as to nuclear war itself, for it holds that if it is just to forbid an intentional action, it is not less just to forbid forming the intention in the first place. If I conceive a plan to kill you and some unforeseen event prevents me from doing this, I am not morally less culpable than if I had actually carried out my plan.

Hence the first in a long series of dilemmas that will confront us in what follows: on the one hand, nuclear deterrence appears to be not only justified but even required by the norms of prudence since it appears to be the only reliable means available to us, under a regime of mutual assured destruction, to avoid nuclear war and to protect national sovereignty; on the other hand, nuclear deterrence appears to be morally unjustified.

The principle of tolerable divergence is no longer satisfied, with all the disastrous consequences that flow from that for the legitimacy of armed force. As a practical matter, the conflict is resolved in favor of prudence, with no further attention being paid to ethical considerations. This is what is called realism.

2.3 The preceding conclusion is nonetheless too hastily drawn, for it rests, in respect of ethics, solely on the norms associated with the institution of defense, which is to say the tradition of just war. Our inquiry needs to be extended to take into account common morality. The difficulty is that common morality is divided between two poles, consequentialism and deontology, whose judgments in particular cases are liable to be profoundly incompatible.

Consequentialism judges an action or a policy by exclusively considering the value that is to be assigned to the consequences of this action or policy for the whole of humanity (or, in an enlarged version, all sentient beings). A just action is one that maximizes this value.

Deontology concerns itself only with the nature of the acts (keeping a promise, lying, committing murder, and so on) that it absolutely prescribes, authorizes, or prohibits, as the case may be, without taking into consideration the value of the consequences.

Moral philosophy treats situations, whether real or hypothetical, in which the conflict between these two dimensions of moral judgment assumes tragic proportions. "Thou shalt not kill" is a deontological imperative that our moral sense enjoins us to obey. But what if, by killing one innocent person, I prevent twenty-two other innocents from being killed? If I truly consider the murder of one innocent person to be abhorrent, then in this case, a consequentialist would say, the categorical prohibition of murder is contrary to reason.

It is especially in sacrificial situations of this type that the two dimensions of common morality disagree most sharply.[6] Nuclear deterrence is no exception. Consequentialist norms justify nuclear deterrence; deontological norms condemn it. The complexity of the debate may be seen in considering this fact alone: the conflict of norms no longer divides only prudence and morality; it divides morality itself.

The tradition of just war ignores consequentialism. The principle of discrimination is plainly deontological in nature, since it refuses to accept that evil (the murder of innocents) can be placed in the service of the good (the cessation of hostilities, for example, which saves lives on both sides). The principle of proportionality, for its part, is interested in consequences, but it does not constitute an independent principle: because it defines a necessary, but by no means sufficient, condition of just military action, it cannot supersede the principle of discrimination. Moreover, unlike consequentialism, it does not prescribe the action or policy that *maximizes* the net value of consequences; it requires only that this value not be negative.

2.3.1 In the case of nuclear deterrence, this indifference to consequentialist norms constitutes not only an inadequacy but a grave error, as the philosopher Gregory Kavka, one of the most penetrating thinkers on the subject, vigorously argued some thirty years ago.[7] Kavka holds that, in a situation of mutual assured destruction, what is required by prudence is also required by morality. Under MAD, morality demands that the general interest of humanity as a whole be maximized—this consequentialist maxim leading to the same judgments and actions as the one that lays down the obligation to maximize the national interest.

It may be that nuclear deterrence is the only means of preventing a conflict from being unleashed whose escalation would lead to cataclysmic disaster for both belligerents. If so, a refusal to form the intention to kill tens of millions of innocent persons would be causally sufficient to produce tens of million murders, again on both sides. When the gap between the consequences of two actions is immensely great—in this case what separates the survival of humanity from its self-annihilation—it would be tragically unreasonable, Kavka concludes, not to adopt a consequentialist criterion.

Sacrificial situations in which consequentialism comes into conflict with deontological norms often have the structure of what is known as Sophie's choice, after the title that William Styron gave to his famous novel. The situation it describes is this: a Nazi officer orders Sophie to choose which of her two children will go to the gas chamber, the other one being spared; if she refuses to choose, both children will perish. What could it mean for Sophie to behave "rationally" (if one may be permitted to apply this terminology to such a gruesome nightmare)? Consequentialism recommends that

Sophie agree to the terms imposed by the Nazi officer and sacrifice one of her children, since at least the other one will live. The structure of the choice is such that the sacrificial solution dominates—in the technical sense this term has in rational choice theory[8]—the nonsacrificial solution: in either case the sacrificed child would die. Nuclear deterrence reinforces the obviousness of consequentialist rationality in this regard. It suffices, in other words, to form an intention to kill N innocents in the enemy's population (where N is a number as large as one likes) in order to prevent not only N individuals in one's own population from being killed but also the N threatened individuals from being killed.

In the two previous chapters I cited to an abundant literature concerning the particular form that the MAD structure assumed during the Cold War. Kavka holds not only that what occurred during this period was consistent with both prudence and consequentialist ethics, but that neither one could have concluded differently than the other. Two counterfactual scenarios can be imagined. What would have happened if the United States had unilaterally disarmed? The Soviet Union might have been tempted to commit nuclear blackmail. In the absence of an American nuclear umbrella, third-party countries, finding themselves suddenly vulnerable to Soviet attack, would have begun to build atomic arsenals. The result might have been a major military conflict, leading in the worst case to global nuclear war. What would have happened, on the other hand, if the United States and the Soviet Union had mutually and simultaneously disarmed? Because nuclear deterrence serves not only to prevent a nuclear conflict but also a conventional war between nuclear powers, disarmament would probably have given rise to such a war. Moreover, paradoxically, the two powers, having disarmed, would have had an incentive to rearm, each in the hope of overtaking the other, making a nuclear conflict more probable. The prudential calculus takes into account only one's own losses; in addition to these, the consequentialist calculus incorporates the losses suffered by one's adversary. It is clear from these alternative scenarios, however, the gains and losses on both sides are registered concurrently.

2.3.2 Can deontological norms be dispensed with altogether? Even Kavka is obliged to recognize the force of what he calls the wrongful intentions principle, strongly rooted in our moral intuitions: it is wrong to form the intention to commit an act if it is wrong to commit this act. Admitting this principle, however, while recognizing the force of the consequentialist argument, leads to an apparently insoluble paradox:

> Let P stand for "cause the deaths of tens of millions of innocent persons."
>
> The consequentialist argument categorically concludes that
>
> 1. It is right to form the intention to P.
>
> Nevertheless, we are intuitively sure that
> 2. It is wrong to P.
>
> Taking into account the wrongful intentions principle,
>
> 3. For all x, it is wrong to form the intention of doing x if doing x is wrong, we are led into contradiction.

This, according to Kavka, is the paradox into which the mere potentiality of mutual assured destruction plunges us. I shall call it the moral paradox of nuclear deterrence. Never in the history of human affairs has the conflict between common morality, which, insofar as it has a deontological or at least a non-consequentialist dimension, is expressed by (3), and consequentialist rationality, which considers (1) to be incontestable, been either as agonizing or as tragic. However much the proponents of deterrence are convinced that (1) is irrefutable and their adversaries convinced of the same with regard to (3), there is reason to suspect that in either case they have grasped only a part of the truth.

The universal truth of (3) has been challenged. Some authors, including Kavka himself, have found themselves reduced to defending the awkward position that this principle is always true, except in the case of nuclear deterrence. One might argue that the intention to P is simply conditional, but this would do nothing to resolve the conundrum. If I form a plan to kill you so long as certain conditions beyond my control are satisfied, the moral status of my intention is the same as if it were unconditional. Nevertheless, it needs to be kept in mind that a deterrent intention is not a conditional intention in the ordinary sense of the term. The conditions that would lead me to P are so little out of my control that what I expect from my intention to P is precisely that these conditions will not be realized. A deterrent intention, to use Kavka's terms, is "self-defeating" or "self-stultifying,"[9] in the sense that only an instrument in the service of a meta-intention contradicts it.

Does this dodge suffice to dispel the moral paradox? Many authors do not think so. Some of them, however, have sought to mobilize principles other than the wrongful intentions principle in order to arrive at the same conclusion—namely, that nuclear deterrence is unjustifiable from the point of view of deontological ethics. Jefferson McMahan has proposed this principle: "It is wrong, other things being equal, to risk doing that which it would be wrong to do."[10] But this maxim does not appear to be sufficiently discriminating. It would tolerate, for example, the notorious doomsday machine we encountered earlier, which, in making nuclear retaliation automatic, without the least possibility of human intervention, has the consequence that no one runs the risk of committing a wrongful act, since there is no longer any question of *acting*.

Deontologists are generally agreed in likening nuclear deterrence to hostage taking. They hold that the taking of hostages is morally reprehensible because (1) it forces innocent persons (2) to run a grave risk (3) without their consent. This is not to be confused with the sometimes morally legitimate case where one threatens someone who shirks a duty. Hostages are third parties, and it is not their behavior that hostage takers seek to influence or constrain. The conditions imposed by hostage takers are typically illegitimate, but this is not what makes the taking of hostages a wrongful act. It is wrong to take a third party hostage in order to force a debtor to reimburse his debt, for example, even though the debtor has an obligation to repay you. In the same way, nuclear deterrence cannot be justified by the fact that the behavior one seeks to impose on an adversary, which is to say nonaggression, is something to which one is morally entitled. Finally, supposing that the hostage taker achieves his purposes and therefore renounces carrying out his threat, this fact cannot render the threat morally acceptable.

2.3.3 Kavka's paradox expresses a *moral dilemma.* A moral dilemma is much more than a conflict between contradictory ethical requirements. A conflict of this sort is ordinarily resolved by weighing, however implicitly or imprecisely, the relative importance of the requirements. Here, however, the paradoxical form of the dilemma rules out any hope of arbitration in the usual sense. Practical reason is shown to be in contradiction with itself. I have suggested that it is in connection with the question of sacrifice (whether individual or collective) that ethics most clearly manifests its internal inconsistency.[11] The moral paradox of deterrence comes under the general head of what may be called sacrificial paradoxes, but it is probably unique in involving not an individual choice but the policy of a public institution on a large scale.

This dilemma is the main trunk from which the various theoretical positions that make up the debate on nuclear deterrence branch off. The scandal caused by the moral paradox has imparted an admirable energy and imagination to a series of attempts to rescue practical reason from the dangers arising, on the one hand, from the disagreement between prudence and morality and, on the other, from the disagreement within morality itself.

We may join Steven Lee in distinguishing three major approaches: prudential revisionism, strategic revisionism, and moral revisionism. With regard to the first, it is a question of showing that prudential reasoning as I have presented it, which argues in favor of nuclear deterrence, is in fact invalid. If this can be done, it would lead to the rejection, rather than the justification, of nuclear deterrence in respect of prudence, which would have a twofold effect. On the one hand, the moral paradox would dissolve since, as we have seen, consequentialist norms cannot but agree with prudential norms, and therefore Kavka's proposition (1) would be proven to be false, and on the other hand, moral judgment, now assured of its correctness in condemning nuclear deterrence, would agree with prudential judgment.

The second approach proceeds in the opposite direction. It seeks to establish that the deontological rejection of nuclear deterrence is the result of an insufficiently thorough and discriminating analysis. On this view, the term *deterrence* needs to be more precisely defined, because it covers two very different options. It is necessary to distinguish between city-targeting strategies, which deliberately aim at civilian populations, and pure counterforce strategies, which aim only at military targets. This second approach attempts to show that certain counterforce strategies can pass the deontological test. If this can be done, then there exists at least one nuclear deterrence strategy that reconciles prudence, consequentialism, and deontology. This is why Lee speaks of strategic revisionism.

If the first two approaches prove to be inadequate, there remains moral revisionism. The first two proceed from a critique of generally accepted arguments and conclusions without calling into question moral norms themselves; the third approach, in order to reconcile prudence and morality, seeks to modify moral norms in such a way that they will be congruent with prudential judgment. Paradoxically, this ad hoc strategy is at once the most radical conceptually and the most conservative politically, since it amounts to justifying the status quo by devising criteria suited to this very purpose.

3. Prudential Revisionism and the Prudential Paradox

Is nuclear deterrence really effective? The prudential argument commonly advanced in support of its effectiveness can be seen, on reflection, to be singularly weak. It rests essentially on the sophism post hoc ergo propter hoc. From 1945 until the present day there has been neither a nuclear conflict nor a conventional war between the two superpowers, nor a third world war. Must we conclude from this that, under a regime of mutual assured destruction, it was *impossible* for such things to happen? Are we justified in inferring from this that, in the absence of nuclear deterrence—if, in other words, the two superpowers were able to rely for deterrence only on their conventional forces—such things *would* have occurred, or would have been more probable? The historical record—what has actually happened—does not allow us to answer questions such as these, which take the form of counterfactual conditionals. Only in the framework of a theory can we hope to find answers or even to formulate questions in the first place.

Advocates of prudential revisionism propose such a theory. They maintain that nuclear deterrence, unlike conventional deterrence, is not justifiable on prudential grounds. Unexpectedly, and in a very interesting fashion, their argument has the form of a paradox, which, following David Gauthier and others, I shall call the prudential paradox.

3.1 The conditions necessary for deterrence to be effective, in general, involve beliefs that the threatening party tries to implant in the mind of the threatened party with a view to influencing its behavior. The threatened party must be made to believe that, if it does not conform to the rule of behavior it is enjoined to respect, the threat will undoubtedly be carried out and that it will suffer grievous damage as a result. Four constituent beliefs may be distinguished. The threatened party must believe that:

> 1. The threatening party is capable of carrying out its threat;

> 2. The threatening party is both willing and determined to carry out its threat;

> 3. If the threatened party behaves as it is asked to do, the threat will not be carried out;

> 4. If it does not behave accordingly, the injury it may be expected to suffer—this injury being calculated by multiplying the magnitude of the harm by its subjectively estimated probability—would be very substantial.

Strategic theory would do well to assess the effectiveness of nuclear deterrence in relation to conventional deterrence in the light of this analysis in terms of beliefs. Here it will be useful to introduce a third term in the comparison, the paradigmatic example of effective deterrence: the criminal justice system and its apparatus of penal sanctions.

There are two essential differences between military deterrence in general and criminal deterrence. In the first case but not in the second, threats are usually reciprocal and the failure of deterrence leads to war. Moreover, military deterrence involves a far more limited number of actors than criminal deterrence, which applies to a nation's entire population. For this reason the known number of failures of military deterrence and of executed threats is very small.

The mutual character of threats means that military deterrence, by comparison with criminal deterrence, fails with regard to the three beliefs (1), (3), and (4). As for belief (1), the threatened party can resort to force in order to neutralize or reduce the threatening party's capacity for carrying out its threat. As for (3), the threatened party has no guarantee that, were it to acquiesce, the threatening party would not attack. In a situation of reciprocal deterrence, each of the two parties may be tempted to strike first, hoping in this way to forestall what it anticipates to be the probable behavior of its adversary. We have considered this configuration at some length in connection with preemption—what Hobbes called *bellum omnium contra omnes* ("war of all against all"). Finally, as for (4), it is enough to note that conventional wars may in general be won, sometimes even with a net positive gain: an adversary's threat, were it to be carried out, therefore does not necessarily entail a prohibitive cost.

Nor, with regard to (2), is the effectiveness of military deterrence very great by comparison with that of criminal deterrence. The reason has to do with the second essential difference between the two types of deterrence, involving the more or less large number of cases where deterrence fails and threats are carried out. The paradox of criminal deterrence is that its success crucially depends on such failures occurring, for they make it clear to anyone who may be inclined to doubt it that the judicial system is in fact determined to apply the sanctions with which it threatens potential offenders. In principle, this paradox affects all institutional systems of deterrence. If the number of failures is too small, deterrence will be ineffective since the expectation that a punishment will be administered in the event of transgression is not strong enough. Accordingly, there exists an optimum level of deterrence beyond which any additional success in deterring transgression, by weakening the factual basis on which the belief in the determination of the criminal justice system to carry out its threats rests, is paid for by a greater failure in some other connection. This optimum, measured by the number of times deterrence fails, is more or less far removed from a society's disruption (or breakdown) threshold. The greater this gap, which I shall call the stability gap, the more stable a society is, all other things being equal.

A nation seeking to defend itself by demonstrating its resolve to punish what it considers to be transgressions of sovereignty seldom has a comparably rich catalogue of precedents at its disposal. It can, however, succeed in making an adversary presume that it is willing to carry out its threats. This presumption will be all the stronger as it is reasonable to believe, assuming a minimal degree of rationality on the part of the threatening party, that it is in its interest to do so. In the case of national defense, carrying out a threat has advantages that are not normally found in the case of a criminal justice system. A nation can thwart the aims of a transgressor, undo what it has done, retake what it has gained. If it emerges victorious from a war that it unleashed by responding to an attack, it may gain more than if it had refrained from responding. Another advantage, this time common to both criminal and military sanctions, is that future transgressors may be deterred. Pioneering work in game theory has confirmed what intuition suggests—namely, that it may be rewarding to apply sanctions that cost you in the short run more than they benefit you if this has the effect of giving you a reputation for toughness that will keep those who might be tempted to attack you at bay.[12] It needs to be kept in mind that this reputation effect has two faces, one, bound up with demonstration effects, looking toward the past; the other, peculiar to presumption effects, looking toward the future. Whereas demonstration effects rely on precedents, presumption effects proceed from reasoning alone, with no reference to past acts. Reputation effects being a matter of common knowledge (each person knows x; everyone knows that everyone else knows x; and so on),[13] an adversary, having taken this effect into account, believes that the threatening power has an interest in punishing transgression, even though doing this would otherwise be unreasonable.

A nation must therefore rely for its defense chiefly on presumption effects. Note, however, that a presumption effect is only an imperfect substitute for a demonstration effect. It is more important for a potential aggressor to be able to anticipate what its adversary would really do if it were to disregard the adversary's warnings than to speculate what a rational person might do under the same circumstances.

3.2 The concepts just introduced in relation to criminal and military forms of deterrence will be helpful in comparing conventional deterrence and nuclear deterrence.

Let us consider the reciprocal character of nuclear deterrence. In a MAD structure, by definition, deterrence assumes a wholly new aspect: mutual vulnerability. Conventional deterrence generally tends to reduce the strength of beliefs (1), (3), and (4); nuclear deterrence, by contrast, gives them renewed vigor. There is no doubt that the adversary has the capability of causing you an immense harm (belief 1). Nor is there any doubt that this harm, even if multiplied only by an extremely small probability, would be so great that it is imperative not to run the risk of its coming to pass (belief 4). These two consequences of MAD are often referred to as the crystal ball effect. In a conventional situation, since the net gains that each party expects from an outbreak of hostilities depend crucially on whether it will be victorious and since each party may be badly mistaken in its expectations, deterrence is fragile: the outcome frequently turns on errors of calculation, assessment, and anticipation that only the unfolding of the conflict itself can reveal. Under MAD, the two adversaries know with absolute certainty, as if the future had been revealed to them by reading a crystal ball, what their mutual destiny will be in the event that the conflict actually occurs.

A third consequence of MAD is likewise to strengthen belief (3). Each party may be assured, with a very high degree of confidence, that the other will not initiate hostilities if it refrains from provoking the other in any way. It is the extreme power of nuclear weapons, the very thing that gives rise to the crystal ball effect, that produces what is known in the literature as the mutual assurance effect. This latter effect is something entirely new in the history of defensive strategic thought. In conventional warfare, beliefs (1) and (3) tend to vary inversely: the more powerful a nation's armed forces, the less assurance there is that it will not be tempted to use them to strike first; here power and provocation go hand in hand. MAD, by contrast, reconciles two essential elements of effective deterrence, power and non-provocation. Mutual assurance results from the fact that each nation knows that the other stands to gain nothing from attacking first, since, in a situation of mutual vulnerability, attacking first not only provides no protection against the destruction of one's own society but actually makes it extremely probable. Mutual assurance is also known as self-deterrence: since to attack would be to commit suicide, the concern for one's own survival makes restraint the highest priority.

The foregoing can be expressed in the language of game theory. In conventional deterrence, the system of beliefs exhibits a "prisoner's dilemma"[14] structure: because neither party rules out the possibility that the other will attack first, each one finds it preferable to do just this. This is the logic of preemption. MAD transforms this structure into a coordination game: the essential interests of the two parties coincide, for it is absolutely necessary that they avoid the fate of mutual annihilation. To be sure, it is an imperfect coordination game to the extent that the possibility of gaining some more or less minor advantage places the two players in a relation of rivalry, where what one wins the other loses. But what is at stake in that case is trivial by comparison with their common interest in not falling into the abyss. The structure that best summarizes this situation is the game of chicken.[15] We have already encountered it in connection with the Cuban Missile Crisis and the dance of death between Kennedy and Khrushchev.

In combination, the crystal ball effect and the mutual assurance effect give nuclear deterrence a very high degree of robustness and stability that conventional deterrence cannot hope to match. The problem is that the very things that produce these two effects produce a third effect, which seems fatal to the effectiveness of nuclear deterrence: it is fundamentally not credible. The belief expressed by (2) has a factual basis neither in demonstration effects nor in presumption effects. The first kind requires precedents, but under the reign of MAD there would no longer be a society left to draw lessons from them. Could the resolve displayed by the threatening party in carrying out nonnuclear threats serve as a substitute? As Lee remarks, it is "as if a government tried to demonstrate its willingness to carry out its legal threat of capital punishment by its diligence in prosecuting parking violators."[16] Presumption effects, for their part, depend on what is understood to constitute the interest of the threatening party. This party could not seriously contemplate, unless it were insane, unleashing a cataclysmic chain of events that would bring ruin upon its own society. Could it be in its interest to sacrifice short-term rationality in order to earn a reputation for toughness? Evidently not, if it must pay for that with the death of its own people.

In conventional deterrence, credibility is not an independent variable. Threats are credible exactly to the extent that military power carries the day. The greater this power, the less damage an adversary will be able to cause in the course of a war, the more reasons the threatening nation has to carry out its threat—and the more credible the threat. Nuclear deterrence, by contrast, has the property of reconciling power and non-provocation, on the one hand, and breaking the traditional link between power and credibility, on the other.

The assessment of nuclear deterrence with regard to prudence therefore runs up against a formidable problem not unlike the moral problem we considered earlier. In that case morality was shown to be in contradiction with itself; here it is prudence that finds itself in the same situation. Not only does nuclear deterrence present both enormous strengths and enormous weaknesses; these things are also intimately related, for they flow from a single source—the vast destructive power of nuclear weapons. The mutual assurance effect amounts to a self-deterrence effect, but self-deterrence evidently entails a crucial problem of credibility. Small wonder that scholars and strategists have arrived at very different conclusions regarding the effectiveness of nuclear deterrence.

3.3 In principle there is a difference in kind between this prudential problem and the moral paradox. The latter assumes the form of a conflict of obligations, whereas the former arises from a tension between two elements constituting a single obligation. It may seem, then, that the prudential problem is only apparently a paradox: it ought to suffice to draw up a balance sheet of pluses and minuses, of pros and cons, in order to determine what prudence requires to be done. Many authors, however, particularly those to whom the question of nuclear deterrence is of interest because it challenges the soundness of rational choice theory, think otherwise.

David Gauthier describes the prudential paradox in the following terms:

> 1. It is rational to make nuclear threats, but it is not rational to carry them out;

> 2. If it is not rational to carry out a threat, it is not rational to make that threat.[17]

Lee proposes a weaker version of this formulation.[18] Proposition (1), in its first part, implicitly acknowledges what accounts for the great superiority of nuclear deterrence, namely, the crystal ball effect; in its second part, (1) recognizes that carrying out a threat is very dangerous. Proposition (2) states the problem of credibility in compressed form: if it is very dangerous and therefore irrational to carry out a threat, then the threat lacks credibility (presumption effect) and so is ineffective; if it is ineffective, then there is no reason to make a threat, and so the threat is irrational. Proposition (1), in other words, says that nuclear deterrence is effective; (2) says that it is not effective. The right approach, then, is to weigh all these factors, both the ones that favor effectiveness and those that argue against it, and to draw up a balance sheet.

There is reason to think that this weaker version misses the essential point. Why is it rational to threaten an enemy with nuclear retaliation, as (1) asserts? Because the threat, to use Kavka's terminology, has autonomous effects—that is, effects independent of the effects produced by carrying out the threat. These autonomous effects are unambiguously positive, since in the event that deterrence succeeds, the enemy refrains from attacking; the effects produced by carrying out the threat, by contrast, are catastrophic. The basis for (1) is the argument that, in considering deterrence from the standpoint of rationality, the autonomous effects must be taken into account; indeed, they are the only ones that come into play when, in the event that deterrence succeeds, the threat is not carried out. By contrast, (2) amounts to affirming that the autonomous effects of a deterrent intention play no role at the moment of decision in the assessment made by the threatening party of the rationality of its threat. To bring out this very subtle point, Kavka devised the following fable, known in the literature as the toxin puzzle.[19]

An eccentric billionaire, who has made his money from applied research in cognitive science, makes you an offer. "You see this vial, it contains a toxin that, if you drink it, will make you sick as a dog for a day but will not kill you or have any lasting effects. If you swallow the contents of this vial, I will pay you a million dollars." You are immediately delighted, thinking that the physical discomfort will be as nothing by comparison with the fortune you stand to make, when the billionaire adds this: "I am not interested whether you actually drink the toxin; all that matters is that you form the intention to drink it. I have brought this machine of my own invention, a brain scanner that is capable of determining the precise nature of your intentions. You will plug it into your brain at midnight tonight and it will record the presence or absence of an intention to drink the toxin tomorrow afternoon. Oh, by the way, I won't even wait for you to drink it before I pay you the money. If the machine detects a positive intention, tomorrow at 10:00 a.m. you will find a million dollars in your bank account." Having gotten your signature on the contract, the billionaire leaves you to collect your thoughts—bitter ones, as it turns out, for as a philosopher of mind, you soon realize that you will never succeed in putting your hands on the pile of money, which at first sight looked to be easily within your reach, or, rather, within reach of your lips.

Kavka invites us to think about the puzzle in the following way. Tomorrow afternoon, whether or not you have found the million dollars in your bank account, not only do you have no reason to drink the toxin, you have a very good reason not to drink it. The past is what it is, and your decision is not going to change it. There exists a dominant strategy,[20] not to drink, and it is the rational strategy. You have known this from the first—and therefore also this evening at midnight. Because forming an intention is not a volitional act, it is impossible for you to form the intention to do x if you know that, when the moment comes, it will be unreasonable for you to do x. It is therefore impossible for you, this evening at midnight, to form the intention to drink the toxin tomorrow afternoon.

The crucial point in all of this is that the subject, to the extent that he is rational, finds himself incapable of taking into account the autonomous effect of the intention to drink, which is to say a gain of one million dollars. If you could form intentions and plans at will, you would unhesitatingly form the intention to drink, since doing so will make you rich at no cost, there being no obligation to drink. But one cannot form the intention to do x if one has no reason to do x and if one has good reasons to refrain from doing x. With regard to nuclear warfare, then, Kavka advances the following argument.[21] It is rational to threaten an enemy with nuclear retaliation, as proposition (1) asserts; but it is not *possible* for a rational subject to make such a threat. This is a way of interpreting proposition (2) in such a way as to make it compatible with (1). But doing this lands us in another paradox, which Kavka formulates thus: nuclear deterrence creates a situation in which a rational subject cannot do the very thing that it is rational for him to do.

This version of Gauthier's prudential paradox appears to be more troublesome still, for it obliges us to abandon what looks like an analytic truth: that which a rational person does is rational. The prudential paradox assumes other forms, which are not obviously themselves equivalent; nor are they equivalent to Gauthier's formulation, either in its original version or as revised by Kavka. The strongest form is the following:

> 3. In order to be effective, nuclear deterrence must be absolutely effective;

> 4. If nuclear deterrence is absolutely effective, then it is not effective.

Let us call this form of the prudential paradox the paradox of self-stultification (in relation to the effectiveness of nuclear deterrence). Proposition (3) expresses the same idea as the second part of Gauthier's proposition (1), only in a more radical way: nuclear deterrence cannot tolerate even a single failure, for one failure by itself would be too many. During the Cold War, many authors made this point in more or less dramatic ways. As Bernard Brodie put it, nuclear deterrence "uses a kind of threat which we feel must be absolutely effective, allowing for no breakdowns ever. The sanction is, to say the least, not designed for repeating action. One use of it will be fatally too many."[22] In the words of Leon Wieseltier, nuclear deterrence "must be the only public arrangement that is a total failure if it is successful only 99.9% of the time."[23] This peculiarity of nuclear deterrence unambiguously distinguishes it from conventional deterrence, where failure may lead to a war that will prove to be advantageous for the threatening party.

Proposition (4), like (2), addresses the problem of credibility. So long as no transgression is punished, deterrence loses all effectiveness, since the demonstration effect is null. Presumption, which in any case cannot compensate for the absence of demonstration, is itself nonexistent since a rational agent could not form the intention to commit an irrational act, in accordance with proposition (2) as revised by Kavka.

The paradox of self-stultification is resolved quite simply by concluding that nuclear deterrence is ineffective: if it were effective, it would be effective absolutely; if it were absolutely effective, it would not be effective. This conclusion can also be arrived at on the basis of the following dilemma. Nuclear deterrence is either

5. a failure generally because it suffers particular failures; or

6. a failure generally because it does not suffer particular failures.

This dilemma can also be expressed by means of a concept we have
previously considered: the breakdown threshold of a society being
equal to zero (i.e., a single failure of deterrence is fatal) and the deterrent optimum being equal at least to one (successful deterrence),
MAD rules out the possibility that stability will be attained.

3.4 Thus the argument on behalf of prudential revisionism. It claims
to reconcile prudence, consequentialism, and deontology by showing that these standards of judgment are unanimous in repudiat-
ing nuclear deterrence. Not everyone agrees, of course. Defenders
of mutual assured destruction maintain that prudential arguments
against nuclear deterrence suffer from disabling logical defects
and seek to provide a rational basis for what common sense urges—
namely, that if war is made to seem sufficiently horrible, it can be
eliminated. They are therefore obliged to defend nuclear deterrence
on moral grounds, which leads them to adopt a strategy of moral
revisionism. I shall examine their arguments last. Let us turn now
to strategic revisionism.

4. Strategic Revisionism

The approach taken by advocates of strategic revisionism consists
in conventionalizing nuclear weapons, as it were. So long as a
counterforce strategy is pursued to the exclusion of any other, they
argue, it is possible to envisage limited nuclear conflicts. A nation
might conceivably emerge the winner from such a conflict, then,
not only in the sense that the enemy has been vanquished, but also
that it finds itself in a better position in the aftermath of the conflict than if it had not occurred. Under these conditions, nuclear
deterrence can be credible and therefore justified from a prudential
standpoint. But it can also be seen to be in conformity with deonto-

logical norms, since it avoids threatening civilians and has no need to take innocents hostage. If this argument could be persuasively made, then strategic revisionism would succeed in reconciling prudence, consequentialism, and deontology in a manner inverse to that of prudential revisionism: there exists at least one form of nuclear deterrence that satisfies all these standards of judgment.

Although strategic revisionism, in the debate over nuclear deterrence, has caused more ink to be spilled by American authors than the other two approaches, I will not dwell on it at undue length. From the theoretical point of view, it is the least interesting of the three. Moreover, it is possible to show that strategic revisionism is doomed to failure. In seeking to graft a model inspired by conventional war onto the dynamic characteristics of nuclear warfare, it actually increases the risk that a nuclear conflict will be unleashed. The fundamental error of this approach is that it fails to recognize the absolutely distinctive feature of nuclear deterrence, which arguably accounts for its superiority—namely, the mutual assurance effect against a first strike. In this respect the arguments of the defenders of MAD are cogent.

4.1 The chief argument against counterforce strategy is that it can be justified from the standpoint of prudence only inasmuch as it is impure (or mixed), which is to say it involves threats against civilians, which in turn makes it deontologically unacceptable. Just so, what would make counterforce strategy justifiable on moral grounds makes it unjustifiable on prudential grounds.

The model of conventional warfare leads those who support counterforce strategy to regard the strength of deterrence as consubstantial with the ability to prevail in an armed conflict; in other words, the best means of deterring an adversary is to threaten it with doing what will be in one's interest to do in the event that deterrence fails and war breaks out. All these are classical notions that nuclear deterrence in a situation of mutual assured destruction spectacularly subverts, but counterforce proponents insist on the necessity of relying on them in order to resolve the prudential paradox. Self-deterrence, which defenders of city-targeting strategies consider a good thing since it assures both parties that a first strike will not be launched, is regarded by counterforce strategists as an unacceptable limitation. The best deterrence is not only that which is exerted *before* a conflict begins—the only kind that proponents of city-targeting strategies contemplate—but above all that which continues to be exerted during the course of a conflict through a dynamic of graduated response. These two types are known as pre-war and intra-war deterrence.

The prudential paradox would vanish if the credibility problem of nuclear deterrence could be resolved. Counterforce strategists claim that it can be. One might argue that they are mistaken, that a counterforce strategy is much less credible—not more credible—than a strategy that aims at the massive destruction of civilian populations. The reason has to do precisely with the logic of intra-war deterrence. For a situation of mutual vulnerability (MAD), counterforce strategy substitutes a situation in which only one side is vulnerable, the side that employs this strategy.[24] The nation in question loses all chance of deterring the enemy from triggering an escalation that would lead to the destruction of its cities. It deprives itself, in other words, of the ability to moderate the behavior of its adversary, dramatically reducing the chances that a nuclear conflict would remain limited. The adversary therefore has no real reason to presume that the nation has the will and the determination to carry out its nuclear counterforce threats. This is the price that must be paid for renouncing what makes nuclear deterrence effective, namely, the assurance of mutual destruction.

4.2 It may nonetheless be thought that an impure counterforce strategy can dispose of the credibility problem. *Impure* signifies a strategy that aims indirectly, or secondarily, at civilian populations, taking military installations near the enemy's urban centers as its main targets. The question that concerns us here is whether such a strategy might resolve the prudential problem. To begin with, however, let us ask whether such a strategy, supposing that it can be justified on prudential grounds, would pass the deontological test. The just war tradition, insofar as it comes under the head of deontological ethics, recognizes what is called the doctrine of double effect. This distinguishes between harm that is intended and must be prohibited, on the one hand, and harm that is unintended but whose occurrence is foreseen as the consequence of an intentional act, on the other. Assuming that an intentional act is morally justified if unintended harm is not taken into account, the presence of such harm, in certain cases, according to the doctrine of double effect, would not alter the moral status of the act. Many authors deny that the doctrine applies in the present case, however.

Their principal argument is the following. It is quite true that the destruction the cities of the nation's adversary are liable to suffer is only indirectly threatened, but the damage is nonetheless intended, since otherwise, counterforce strategy would not be effective. As Walter Stein emphasized more than fifty years ago, "I cannot morally dissociate myself from what I want, from what I cannot avoid wanting as a means to achieving my purpose, if in fact I choose to achieve my purpose by these means."[25] It is therefore wrong to pursue a policy of deterrence if one believes that it can be effective only insofar as it involves threats against civilian populations; whether the threat is direct or indirect matters not at all.

To this it may be replied, of course, following a line of reasoning we examined earlier, that the end sought by making a threat may differ from the end sought by carrying out the threat. If a nuclear conflict should break out, the destruction of urban centers will serve no purpose and therefore is not to be desired in and of itself. It is desirable only to the extent that, prior to the conflict, it strengthens the deterrent effect.

Nevertheless, this objection does not do justice to what sets counterforce strategy apart from other strategies: the fact that the deterrent effect exists only insofar as it can be prolonged after a conflict has begun. In a limited nuclear war, if such a thing is possible, the city-targeting dimension of an impure counterforce strategy would play a decisive deterrent role. Robert Jervis refers in this connection to the logic of hostage-taking. The killing of a few hostages, one by one, makes the prospect of more being killed more credible.[26]

In the eyes of the many critics of counterforce strategy, at least, strategic revisionism is bound to collapse of its own weight: either counterforce strategy is pure and so is not effective, or it is impure and so is not justified from the deontological point of view. Here the tension between prudential and ethical imperatives reaches its highest point. The failure of strategic revisionism—and this is not the least of the ironies we encounter in this regard—is due to exactly what the proponents of counterforce strategy claim to be its chief advantage: the logic of intra-war nuclear deterrence.

4.3 One further point remains to be examined. It is possible that an impure form of counterforce strategy, while failing to supply a sound basis for strategic revisionism, might also undermine prudential revisionism. This would be the case if it could be shown that an impure version is sufficiently more effective than a pure version of counterforce strategy that the conclusion drawn by the proponents of prudential revisionism no longer follows. For if an impure version turned out to be more effective than conventional deterrence, then nuclear deterrence would pass the prudential test—and therefore the consequentialist test as well—while flunking the deontological test. In that case the only way out would be moral revisionism.

Yet this argument is far from being unanimously approved. Convinced proponents and opponents of nuclear deterrence are united in rejecting it. The former are determined to defend nuclear deterrence by appealing to what sets it apart from any alternative, namely, the MAD structure; the latter appeal to the objections raised on various grounds by prudential revisionism.

The principal obstacle to be overcome if recourse to moral revisionism is to be avoided, quite obviously, is the lingering problem of credibility. On the one hand, as we saw earlier, in section 4.1, a pure counterforce strategy is not credible because it prohibits itself from responding in the final stages of an atomic escalation. On the other hand, counterforce strategists hold that the threat of responding to an attack aimed at military targets by retaliation against urban centers likewise has no credibility: in a situation of mutual assured destruction, it would be wholly irrational. The lack of credibility is therefore a result of limiting the response to a level of attack that is either too high or not high enough. This is the principal motivation for the doctrine of flexible response. It is a matter of being able and determined to respond at every level in a proportional and graduated manner.

The main criticism of this doctrine is that, in reverting to the model of conventional war and deterrence, it reinstates the traditional relationship between the three vertices of the golden triangle of deterrence while at the same time exacerbating the tensions of deterrence associated with the extreme destructive power of nuclear weapons. These three vertices, as we have seen, are power, non-provocation (or mutual assurance), and credibility. Credibility implies a sufficient degree of power, but too much power constitutes a provocation and prevents the mutual assurance effect against a first strike from making itself felt.

The argument, more precisely, runs as follows. Deterrence in a MAD situation can be credible only if it rests on mistaken beliefs. A nation must wrongly believe that it is capable of overcoming its own vulnerability; otherwise it must try to make its enemy believe that it believes that. The nation in question, in other words, must believe that it is capable of winning a limited nuclear war and that, as a consequence, it can permit itself the luxury of provocation and venture to initiate an escalation that would be to its advantage. If the nation's enemy does not believe that it believes this, the plausibility of the threat will not be assured; if the enemy does believe that the nation believes this, then its best option is to go ahead and strike first. The strategy therefore proves not to be credible, and so dramatically increases the probability of a nuclear conflict. Accordingly, the doctrine of graduated response is not capable of justifying nuclear deterrence on prudential grounds.

5. Mutual Assured Destruction and Moral Revisionism

The threat of mutual assured destruction, its advocates maintain, can be justified by exploiting its two greatest assets: the unprecedented power of nuclear weapons and the dual manifestation of this power in the form of the crystal ball effect and the self-deterrence effect. City-targeting strategy and the risk of massive destruction to which it subjects tens, indeed hundreds of millions of innocent persons constitute the essence of nuclear deterrence. In the view of prudential revisionism, this leads to a problem of credibility that is fatal for the effectiveness of MAD. What the advocates of prudential revisionism fail to grasp is that from the fact of mutual vulnerability, this fact being a matter of common knowledge,[27] it follows that there is no need to resolve the credibility problem in order to establish the effectiveness of nuclear deterrence. For what results from the fact of mutual vulnerability, which is to say the effect of mutual assurance against a first strike, together with the crystal ball effect, constitutes a sufficient guarantee of effectiveness.

"We shall by a process of supreme irony," Winston Churchill observed in a famous speech delivered before the House of Commons in March 1955, "have reached a stage in this story where safety shall be the sturdy child of terror, and survival the twin brother of annihilation."[28] On this view, terror is the mother of wisdom. The simple idea that war cannot take place if the power to destroy becomes sufficiently great has been formulated in a number of sophisticated ways in the meantime. Let us consider a few of them.

5.1 Not all advocates of mutual assured destruction are of the opinion, as John F. Kennedy put it, that the only choice it offers is "holocaust or humiliation."[29] If a nation is the victim of a limited nuclear strike, it has the option of responding in kind, with another limited strike, in the hope of keeping the conflict within manageable bounds. What defenders of MAD-based strategies deny is that it is possible to obtain any military advantage whatever from a confrontation of this type. The only value of a limited response is deterrent. Like the proponents of counterforce strategies, some proponents of MAD therefore believe that intra-war nuclear deterrence may be possible. Note, however, that the logic of this sort of deterrence does not involve the (false) belief that one of the parties could gain the upper hand through aggression. The logic is entirely different.

Proponents of counterforce strategy, as we have seen, assume that the structure of beliefs is identical with that of the prisoner's dilemma, where taking the initiative constitutes the dominant strategy.[30] Proponents of MAD see the matter in terms of imperfect coordination. In order to avoid a holocaust, the two enemies have no other option than to coordinate their behavior. If the conflict between them amounted "simply" to a clash of wills, including above all the will to survive, then reaching an agreement would not pose a major conceptual problem. What makes the contest so very risky, as we have also seen, is that the two parties are rivals by virtue of the fact that they desire the same things. Each one must not only deter the other from delivering a first nuclear strike but also prevent it from doing the very things it wishes to do itself (invade the territory of a third-party nation, extend ideological influence, and so on) by means of conventional warfare. We are therefore led to distinguish two forms of stability aimed at by nuclear deterrence: crisis stability, which comes from eliminating the risk of a nuclear conflict, and noncrisis stability, which comes from deterring the enemy from attacking by nonnuclear means. Crisis stability rests on the supreme interest that both rivals share—avoiding mutual annihilation. Noncrisis stability is achieved by preventing the conflict between their secondary interests from becoming bellicose. The risk is that, in seeking to guarantee noncrisis stability, nuclear deterrence imperils crisis stability.

Robert Jervis, a leading advocate of MAD, has extended a line of argument originally proposed by Thomas Schelling.[31] To be sure, the credibility of nuclear retaliation against a first attack, whether conventional or taking the form of a limited nuclear strike, is not a priori sufficiently strong to resolve the prudential problem. It is nonetheless not zero. Instead it is, as Jervis puts it, middling. The related chance that a nuclear conflict will remain limited is middling as well—sufficiently small that the threat of mutual destruction must still be taken very seriously but sufficiently great that each party may be tempted to carry out its threat of a limited response— not because each party hopes to gain the upper hand in this process of escalation (as in the case of counterforce strategy), but because in this way it ratchets up a notch the risk of mutual destruction while

at the same time increasing the pressure that it exerts on its adversary to be the first one to disengage from the process of escalation.
Each step in the process, considered by itself, is an irrational ges-
ture, obliging the party that takes it to run unacceptable risks. But it
may be reasonable if one takes into account the effects that it has on
tho cyotom of boliofo: tho advoroary, bolioving that it io doaling with
a reckless enemy, will prefer to act prudently. Nevertheless, we must
analyze the problem at a deeper logical level. Let us suppose that
the theory I have just described, according to which it is rational to
behave irrationally, is a matter of common knowledge: each party
knows that even if the other is rational, it has an interest in simulating the behavior of an irrational actor. Even if it were scarcely
credible a priori, because wildly irrational, that the other would risk
embarking on a course of escalation, this possibility must be treated
with the utmost seriousness. A nuclear threat, even one that is only
modestly credible, may yet be highly effective.

The appeal of this line of reasoning has been greatly strengthened
by certain advances in the theory of repeated games with imperfect
information, where the uncertainty bears upon the rationality of
the players.[32] In a repeated game of chicken, in which the fact that
the players are rational is not a matter of common knowledge, there
exist equilibria that render a player's threat of causing irreparable
damage effective if the status quo that favors him is not maintained.
These equilibria are made possible by a reputation effect involving
the belief that one's adversary is irrationally disposed to carry out
its threats. Note that here the presumed irrationality is mutual. In
counterforce strategy, by contrast, only one side is considered to be
irrational, the one that militarily is the weaker of the two.

5.2 By far the most conceptually interesting defense of MAD, if not
the most convincing one from a practical standpoint, is nonetheless
of an altogether different kind. It rests on a distinction between two
types of nuclear threat: on the one hand, the threat to act intention-
ally in responding to an act of aggression; on the other, the threat to
make no attempt to control the course of escalation.[33] I shall speak
in the first case of intentional threats and in the second, for rea-

sons that will shortly become apparent, of existential threats. The difference between the two types of threat is of the same nature, philosophically, as the one that separates an intention from the prediction of one's own conduct. Thus, for example, I can foresee that, in a fit of anger, I will cause damage, without having had any intention either to become angry or to cause such damage. The second type of threat comes under the head of this same faculty, by which we are able to stand outside ourselves, as it were, looking upon ourselves from the point of view of another person.

It is very unlikely that a nuclear conflict would remain limited, resisting a process of escalation that will lead the two parties into mutual annihilation. It is exactly this, I repeat once more, that deprives nuclear threats of any real credibility. But this time it is necessary to speak more precisely, making it clear that the lack of credibility attaches to intentional nuclear threats. This very fact, however, according to defenders of MAD-based strategies, makes the existential threat very effective. Again, to be clear, this is not to say that the effectiveness of an existential threat makes it credible, because credibility presupposes a deliberate act, an intention to do something, which is precisely what is not assumed here. An adversary is not deterred because it considers the other's intentional threats to be credible, but because it believes that the mere existence of the colossal arsenal of weapons stockpiled by the enemy to carry out its intentional threats creates a grave risk—of an uncontrollable process of escalation leading to mutual annihilation—that can be moderated only by extreme vigilance.

If the proponents of mutual assured destruction are right, it is easier to understand the fundamental error committed by strategic revisionism in relying on counterforce strategy. This strategy is dangerous because, in order to provide a basis for the credibility of intentional threats, it seeks to make the prospect of a limited nuclear war credible, which could only postpone the possibility of an unlimited escalation escaping the control of the actors, whereas it is the uncertainty (later I shall speak of indeterminacy) attaching to this possibility that is the supreme guarantee of the effectiveness of nuclear deterrence. A limited attack is not deterred by making the threat of a limited response highly credible; it is deterred by keeping the probability of mutual annihilation at a moderate level.

As Daniel Ellsberg has argued, the mere existence of nuclear arsenals that jointly constitute a regime of mutual assured destruction made the doomsday machine of Kubrick's imagination a reality.[34] The automatic character of the machine's response in case of attack is embodied by the prospect of a process of escalation that becomes autonomous, which is to say uncontrollable. David Lewis, writing almost thirty years ago, emphasized that "our military capabilities [are what] matter, not our intentions or incentives or declarations. . . . You don't tangle with tigers—it's that simple."[35] Both sides, Steven Lee observes, worry that they "would be up against a monster, an inhuman process of potentially inexorable escalation." All this takes us far beyond the realm of strategy, which assumes at least two agents freely interacting with each another. If one can speak of rationality here, it is "the kind of rationality in which the agent contemplates the abyss and simply decides never to get too close to the edge."[36]

This interpretation of the deterrent capability of MAD is only partially compatible with the argument developed on the basis of a reputation effect in a repeated game of chicken—an argument that is strategic in the highest degree. According to the existential interpretation of nuclear threats, it would be exceedingly risky to join a battle where each side seeks to display greater will and determination than the other. Of the four conditions that are supposed by prudential revisionism to be necessary conditions of successful deterrence, the second, having to do with the will of the threatening party, is sidelined by MAD: the belief regarding capability and power renders it useless.

Thus the defenders of mutual assured destruction claim to have resolved the prudential paradox. Their argument purports to show that it may sometimes be rational to threaten even though it would be irrational to carry out the threat. In making an intentional threat, one implicitly makes an existential threat, and this existential threat may be effective even if carrying out the intentional threat would be irrational.

If they are right, the defenders of mutual assured destruction have succeeded in refuting prudential revisionism: nuclear deterrence is justified in respect of prudence and therefore in respect of consequentialism as well. It now remains for them to find a way of resolving the moral paradox. This they hope to do by means of moral revisionism, which is to say by adapting our moral judgments to the context created by the existence of a situation of mutual assured destruction.

5.3 The conception of nuclear deterrence advanced by the defenders of MAD, in terms of existential threats, makes it possible, they assert, not only to respond to the problem of credibility, by showing that it does not arise, but also to devise an elegant solution to the moral dilemma. Deterrent intention has been objected to on two grounds: on the one hand, not only is its rationality suspect, but the possibility of forming such an intention may be doubted and therefore its very existence as well; on the other, it is accused of being immoral, because it cannot be justified in respect of deontology. Against these two charges there can be but one defense—namely, that there is no need for deterrent intention in order to make nuclear deterrence effective.

David Lewis has forcefully expressed this view, but without either removing its paradoxical character or making a wholly satisfactory argument in its favor: "It is not intentions but capacities that deter. . . . Our war plans are part of our capacities, even when they are not part of our intentions."[37] It would therefore be possible to form a plan to do something even though one has no intention of acting on it. Formulations of this sort do not obviously go beyond the enigmatic notion to which Kavka, in setting forth his paradox, gave the name of a self-defeating (or self-stultifying) intention.

However this may be, even supposing it were clear what is being talked about here, can the deontological test be said to have been satisfied by showing that it is irrelevant? Many authors say no. They wonder whether it really makes sense to argue, as George Quester does,[38] that, just as nuclear weapons have taught us to understand the meaning of the "rationality of irrationality," they must teach us to understand the meaning of the "morality of immorality"—in the event, the morality of a plan that involves, albeit unintentionally, the possibility that tens of millions of innocent persons may perish under abominable conditions. One may be forgiven for suspecting this is a mere sophism.

Critics of moral revisionism put forward the same argument advanced by the critics of strategic revisionism. An impure counterforce strategy fails the deontological test because the murder of civilians, even if it is only foreseen and not directly aimed at, is held to be indispensable in obtaining the desired result, namely, successful deterrence. Even if these deaths are wished for only as a means to an end, they are nonetheless wished for. This conclusion is hardly invalidated by saying that an uncontrollable process is "responsible" for so great a slaughter. It is hoped that this process will escape our control, since it is considered to be the only way to make nuclear deterrence effective.

5.4 Critics of mutual assured destruction obviously do not stop there. They deny that a city-targeting strategy can claim to pass the prudential test, supposing that they have thereby refuted prudential revisionism. They deny that nuclear deterrence is effective or, in any case, more effective than conventional deterrence.

I will limit myself here to what seems to be the strongest argument that can be made in this connection. To the same extent that nuclear deterrence succeeds in guaranteeing crisis stability, it is rendered powerless to guarantee noncrisis stability and vice versa. Each form of instability may be fatal, since each may lead to a nuclear war: directly, in the case of crisis instability; indirectly, in the case of noncrisis stability.

This argument evidently runs up against the doctrine of extended deterrence (the so-called nuclear umbrella), which assumes that crisis and noncrisis stability vary in the same direction, so that the potential for violence at the highest level makes itself felt at all lower levels. Jervis, writing in 1989, well summarized this doctrine: "Second-strike capacity can protect Europe and the Persian Gulf because the Soviets realize that even a conventional, let alone a nuclear, war could easily escalate, but escalation is not so certain as to make the Soviets confident that the West would not dare to use force to resist their predations."[39]

Critics of MAD maintain that this argument is flawed. If your aim is to eliminate the possibility of a nuclear conflict, it will be very difficult to reduce the risk of a conventional war spinning out of control and leading to a nuclear war. The converse is no less true. The reason for this is that the factors that produce the one type of stability are incompatible with those that produce the other type. No matter how sophisticated the strategic reasoning brought to bear, these critics insist, no matter how refined the relevant distinctions may be, there is no escape from what is only a new variation on the theme of the prudential paradox. Here it will be helpful to recall the argument made on behalf of prudential revisionism. In order to demonstrate the superiority of nuclear deterrence over conventional deterrence, one would have to be able to show that the probability of nuclear deterrence failing, ε, is so small that the product εN, where N measures the extent of the damage caused by this failure, is minimized by nuclear deterrence. Given that N, in the case of nuclear deterrence, may be of the greatest magnitude—the destruction of one's own society—it follows that nuclear deterrence must in every respect be shown to be superior to conventional deterrence in minimizing ε. The impossibility of achieving both a very high degree of crisis stability and a very high degree of noncrisis stability dashes all hopes of arriving at this result, however.

In order to establish this impossibility, it is necessary first to take seriously the argument advanced by the advocates of MAD on behalf of city-targeting strategies, but then to turn against them the argument that both advocates and critics of MAD make against counterforce strategies. Briefly stated, the situation is this.

The advocates of MAD claim that nuclear deterrence, relying solely on the crystal ball effect and the mutual assurance (or self-deterrence) effect, guarantees crisis stability without having the least need for what in any case it cannot claim to possess, namely, a high degree of credibility. Even supposing that this lack of credibility is not detrimental to crisis stability, however, it is fatal to noncrisis stability. Under a regime of mutual assured destruction, noncrisis stability can be guaranteed only by a credible threat that one will respond to a conventional act of aggression with a limited nuclear strike, as part of a counterforce strategy. Conversely, if what one wants to guarantee is noncrisis stability, it would be necessary to resort to a counterforce strategy, which would increase the chance that the adversary would make the first move.

In the language of game theory, this amounts to saying that one has to choose between reasoning in terms of a prisoner's dilemma and reasoning in terms of a game of chicken—and all the more so since this choice is a matter of common knowledge. One must choose, in other words, between a Hobbesian war, which each adversary hopes to win but which traps both of them in the logic of preemption, or a regime of self-deterrence, which temporarily postpones the immediate danger while reducing each of the adversaries to a state of impotence in the face of the other's minor provocations.

It is necessary to choose: either Scylla or Charybdis.

Provisional Conclusion

It will come as a surprise that the stumbling block confronting any assessment of nuclear deterrence should turn out to be the prudential problem. Realists think that the profound moral dilemmas presented by nuclear deterrence, which they consider to be purely academic, need not be taken seriously. Yet they cannot remain indifferent to the fact that there is no unanimous response to the question whether nuclear deterrence is effective; that there is no argument that does not provide support for a contrary argument; that there is no line of reasoning that does not take the form of a paradox. From the point of view of reason, this is a source of immense frustration, if not actually humiliation.

Nevertheless, one ought not be unduly surprised. The question whether nuclear deterrence can be justified on prudential grounds is not an empirical question. Any answer to this question must appeal to a *theory* of prudence and rationality. The uncertainty that affects prudential judgments concerning nuclear deterrence is a theoretical uncertainty, amounting perhaps to indeterminacy. We do not know which theory permits us to judge.

The most reductive form of argumentation in this regard is the claim, all too often made, that obviously nuclear deterrence is effective *because* no nuclear war has so far taken place. This reasoning is no less feeble than that of a man on a train who is in the habit of spraying elephant-repellent from the window of his compartment. The proof that doing this removes the danger of an unexpected collision with an elephant crossing the tracks, he believes, is that he has never seen one.[40]

If we are to be able to make progress in thinking about nuclear war, there is no option but to resort to philosophy. The invasive ideology of Big Data, which spreads like a cancer today in the social sciences—if we go on accumulating data, we will be able to dispense with theory—stumbles miserably when it comes up against the obstacle of nuclear war. If a nuclear war were to occur, there will be no data to be collected either from the past—because we will no longer be here to collect them—or from the future—because the future, owing to its indeterminacy, *gives* us nothing. Hubris, in its modern form, prompts us to believe that we can "construct" the future—that whether or not we will perish in a nuclear holocaust depends on us alone. This is a fatal mistake. We can *hope* that we will not perish. The future may have other ideas, however.

If we are to survive, we cannot avoid the necessity of making the future our central preoccupation. And in order to do this, we must enter into metaphysics.

Four

Metaphysical MAD

The future is inevitable, precise, but it may not happen. God
keeps watch in the intervals.

JORGE LUIS BORGES
"The Creation and P. H. Gosse"

Is It Reasonable to Be Rational?

In the preceding chapter I have summarized more than ten thousand pages devoted to strategic thinking about nuclear war and its
culmination in the concept of mutual assured destruction. I could
not have done it without the aid of Steven P. Lee's remarkable book.
This kind of analytic philosophy, rather similar to what one finds in
rational choice theory, is not easy to read, but making the effort is indispensable. Much of what has been written about the atomic threat
amounts to little more than idle chatter because it fails to grasp the
complexity of the conceptual distinctions involved. The critical perspective of the first two chapters, which I adopt once more in this
final chapter, will allow us to treat the subject with the clarity and
rigor it requires.

The dryness of almost all writing on this subject makes us forget
that what we are really talking about, hidden behind so much abstraction, is the atrocities of a war that, were it ever to occur, would
be beyond our power to imagine. What is more, the analytical tools

devised at institutions such as the RAND Corporation—birthplace of rational choice theory and the prisoner's dilemma game—give the impression that the theory of mutual assured destruction is the height of rationalism, when in fact it involves the maddest of human follies.

For having taken MAD theorizing seriously, I was recently accused of making "the major mistake made by most Cold War theorists, in assuming that the world of human affairs is rational."[1] My accuser went on to catalogue the passions that poison human relations, especially in times of war: hatred, envy, jealousy, resentment, the thirst for vengeance, weakness of will, and so on. He concluded that we are "imperfect, intrinsically fallible," and therefore irrational. By way of reply, I observed that he was much more of a rationalist than I am, for inferring irrationality from imperfection assumes that rationality implies perfection: if we were rational, we would be immunized against these destructive passions. This is a great deal to grant to rationality, and all the more as the rationality in question is the paltry one postulated by strategic thought and the theory of *homo oeconomicus*. It amounts to believing that if we were rational in this sense, nuclear deterrence would be effective and atomic peace guaranteed. This makes rationality a sort of ideal, unattainable in our postlapsarian world, of course, but desirable nonetheless. Nothing could be more false.

One can be rational in this sense and in the name of rationality commit abominable acts. We have seen how far nuclear deterrence has exacerbated the tension between deontology and consequentialism, to the point of making them antagonists. It is instructive to recall the religious source of this schism, the biblical story of Caiaphas's choice. Caiaphas, who was high priest of the Jews that year, said to the other chief priests and the Pharisees about Jesus, "You know nothing at all; you do not understand that it is expedient for you that one man should die for the people, and that the whole nation should not perish" (John 11:49–50). Putting Jesus to death is a dominant strategy in the sense this term has in rational choice theory. Jesus is but one Jew: whether he is sacrificed or not, he dies, either as a scapegoat or as one of many casualties in the general

destruction of his people. The rational choice is plainly to acquiesce in his death sentence, even though he is known to be innocent.
Why, then, does this conclusion, *as a matter of principle*, horrify us
today?[2]

One can charge the pure theory of MAD, in the form that I have
presented it, with being a paragon of rational thought and deduce
from this that it is completely unrealistic, as my critic has done
(along with many experts in the field), only at the price of a deplor-
able blindness. The theory ceaselessly runs up against obstacles
that it calls paradoxes, as if it recognized the impossibility of reaching any conclusion. At the very heart of one of its key concepts, the
credibility of a nuclear threat, it places madness. Finally it arrives
at the notion of existential deterrence, which, as we have seen (and
will see in further detail in the present chapter), dispenses with intentions, plans, and strategy. This amounts to something very much
like the opposite of calculating thought.

A word concerning method. There are at least two ways of going
beyond the pure theory of MAD. The first is to formulate an internal
critique, which is to say by making use of the very instruments that
the theory employs. This means applying the basic concepts of rational choice theory and game theory. In setting forth the pure theory
of MAD, I have tried to keep this conceptual apparatus to a bare
minimum. That is impossible in developing the internal critique,
however, and so I have decided to relegate it to an appendix. There
is no need for readers to concern themselves with the details of this
critique in order to follow my argument to its conclusion.

The alternative, to which the present chapter is devoted, is to
develop an external critique, drawing on a wide range of sources
in addition to philosophy and metaphysics: current affairs, history,
anthropology, theology, literary theory. Everything is grist for our
mill in thinking about the time that is left to us before the inevitable
occurs—or doesn't.

The Violence of the Tiger

From the pure theory of MAD, we may retain a negative conclusion. A priori reasoning shows that nuclear deterrence does not work, and this for two reasons. The first is that the threat of retaliation is not credible. The second involves the prudential paradox (or the paradox of self-stultification): for deterrence to succeed, it has to work perfectly; but if it works perfectly, it fails. Nuclear powers are therefore incapable of deterring one another.

Reasoning in the same fashion, how can we extricate ourselves from the prudential paradox, so that nuclear deterrence remains effective *in theory*? Of all the answers to this question that we have considered, the most promising—but also the most daring, for it undermines the most basic assumptions of military thought since the dawn of time—is the doctrine of existential deterrence.

Recall that, on this view, there is no need of any deterrent intention in order to assure the effectiveness of nuclear deterrence. The mere existence of two deadly arsenals pointed at each other, without the least threat of their use being made or even implied, is enough to keep the warheads locked away in their silos. "The existence of a nuclear retaliatory capability suffices for deterrence," as Gregory Kavka puts it, "regardless of a nation's will, intentions, or pronouncements about nuclear weapons use."[3] The insistence on the causal power of the mere existence of a nuclear arsenal has the effect of diminishing the importance of strategy, intentions, plans—in short, the fundamental elements of military doctrine. If there is no need to threaten an adversary, it is because the weapons themselves, due to their extraordinary power, speak for us.

How exactly does existential deterrence work? Who or what deters whom? The explanations given by two leading theorists, David K. Lewis and Bernard Brodie, involve nonhuman actors. Lewis, as we have already seen, invokes the violence of a wild animal. The apparent banality of his formulation conceals a deep insight: "You don't tangle with tigers. It's as simple as that."[4] The implication is that the contest is no longer between two human adversaries. It now has an altogether different form. Neither adversary is in a position to deter the other in a credible way, and yet each one wants and needs to be deterred. The way out of the impasse lies in their jointly imagining a fictitious entity that will deter both of them at the same time—a brilliant solution. Now the contest is between one actor, humanity, whose survival hangs in the balance, and its double, which is to say its own violence exteriorized in the form of a wild animal. The fictitious animal we had better not tangle with is nothing other than the violence that is within us but that we project outside ourselves. It is as if we were threatened, but also protected, by some external force whose power of destruction is infinitely greater than anything nature can threaten us with, but with no more malice toward us than an earthquake or a tsunami.

According to René Girard, the sacred came into being through the operation of a similar mechanism of self-externalized violence.[5] It used to be said of the atomic bomb, especially during the years of the Cold War, that it was our new sacrament. Very few among those who were given to saying this sort of thing saw it as anything more than a vague metaphor. But in fact there is a very precise sense in which the bomb and the sacred can both be said to contain violence in the twofold sense of the verb *to contain*: to have within and to keep in check. The sacred holds back violence by violent means, originally through sacrifice. In the same way, throughout the Cold War, it was as though the bomb had protected us from the bomb. The very existence of nuclear weapons seemed to have prevented a nuclear holocaust, without ceasing to be what made it possible.

One must not come too near to the sacred for fear of unleashing the violence it contains, nor should one stand too far away from it, however, for it secures us against this same violence. Likewise, we must not come too near to the nuclear tiger lest it devour us, nor should we stand too far away from it lest we lose sight of it, for its ferocity shelters us against our own cruelty. The art of deterrence is a matter of finding the right distance from the ravenous beast.

During the Cold War, as Robert McNamara emphasized more than once, the world came within an inch of nuclear apocalypse at least two dozen times.[6] It was not deterrence that saved humanity from extinction, he says; "We lucked out." But is this really true?

Looking at the matter more closely, ought we not say that it was exactly this repeated flirting with the tiger, this series of doomsdays that did not occur, that shielded us from the danger created by our own incuriosity, self-satisfaction, indifference, cynicism, stupidity—in a word, the blissful belief that we will be spared the worst?

The force referred to in Christian theology by the ancient Greek word *katéchon* (literally, that which holds back or restrains) and associated more recently with the work of the German philosopher Carl Schmitt[7] is what slows the march toward apocalypse. For Girard, the katéchon par excellence is the Satan of the Bible, the one of whom it is said "Satan casts out Satan" (Mark 3:23–27). Here Satan represents the principle of self-regulating violence: violence is capable of projecting itself outside itself in an act of self-transcendence and, from this external vantage point, of limiting its own baleful effects. Nuclear deterrence, in the pure form of mutual assured destruction, is the supreme secular incarnation of this logic. All the paradoxes we considered in the previous chapter can now be reinterpreted in accordance with it.

The violence of the tiger is an innocent violence, part of nature. It is, as Rousseau saw, foreign to evil.[8] The nuclear tiger does not have this guilelessness. It owes its existence to an extremely risky decision—namely, to unleash the violence of human beings and their engines of death while counting on the capacity of violence for self-regulation to protect us against annihilation. This is truly a pact with the devil. Hannah Arendt and Günther Anders understood this irresponsible *Gelassenheit*[9] better than anyone else. Both of them, Arendt in connection with Auschwitz, Anders with Hiroshima, described a new regime of evil that deepened the chasm between the casual thoughtlessness of human beings and the gigantic scale of the harm that they are capable of causing. Returning from Hiroshima in 1958, Anders wrote, "At the very moment when the world becomes apocalyptic, and this owing to our own fault, it presents the image . . . of a paradise inhabited by murderers without malice and victims without hatred. Nowhere is there any trace of malice, there is only rubble."[10]

The Force of Destiny

In March 2016, many people snorted with derision when Donald
Trump, then the frontrunner for the Republican Party's nomination,
was pressed to say publicly that he would not use nuclear weapons
in Europe. "I'm not going to use nuclear," he replied finally, "but I'm
not taking any cards off the table."[11]

These people reacted as though there were a contradiction in
what Trump said. "So, will you use nuclear weapons or won't you?
You have to decide one way or the other." There is no contradiction,
in fact; in order to understand why, however, there is no avoiding rational metaphysics, a philosophical discipline that Trump certainly
knows nothing about but that will be essential in what follows.

To say that I will never do x because the circumstances that
would lead or oblige me to do it will never occur is not necessarily
incompatible with saying that I might do it if the circumstances in
question were to occur—unless one assumes a temporal metaphysics such as that of the Megarian School and holds the future to be
necessary, which implies that every possible event will inevitably
occur: if an event never occurs, this is because it is impossible. Now,
Trump did not and could not mean that it was impossible that he
would launch a nuclear first strike. An ethics that would judge the
simple fact of making a nuclear holocaust possible to be an abominable crime therefore cannot be satisfied with the assurance that
this will never happen.

We have already encountered this question twice. The French
doctrine of deterrence, known as deterrence of the strong by the
weak, imagines that it has found a way to escape ethical condemnation by means of a similar logical contortion. More than one
president of the French Republic has said, in effect,[12] "It is precisely
because I have formed a firm intention to kill sixty million innocents that the circumstances that would lead me to act on this intention will not occur." Did he mean by this that it is impossible
for them to occur? In that case the effectiveness of deterrence is
reduced to zero. In the matter of deterrence, it would appear, ethics
and rationality cannot both be satisfied.

In the second chapter, discussing the historic meeting between Reagan and Gorbachev at Reykjavik, in October 1986, I left un-answered the question Gorbachev could have asked Reagan: why would you go on constructing an antimissile shield in this world that we both desire to bring about, a world in which there will no longer be either atomic weapons or the intercontinental missiles used to deliver them? "Of course, you're right," Reagan might have replied (if he were a philosopher), "but there is another possible world near to ours, in which, even though such weapons no longer exist, the threat that they carried with them still exists and MAD continues to hover above the earth, borne aloft by dark clouds." The threat is no longer that of a first strike but of a race to be the one who rearms first. The fact that weapons no longer exist does not prevent the know-how needed to build them from surviving. One must therefore protect oneself against this prospect, either by means of the paradoxical form of deterrence that Jonathan Schell called weaponless deterrence[13] or by an antimissile shield.

It is impossible to escape the necessity of dealing with one of the most difficult of all questions, which the threat of nuclear apoca-lypse renders more problematic than ever: the reality of the future. I will take as my point of departure an observation by Bernard Brodie regarding existential deterrence, which is the temporal counterpart of Lewis's tiger:

> It is the curious paradox of our time that one of the foremost factors making deterrence really work and work well is the lurking fear that in some massive confrontation crisis it may fail. Under these circumstances *one does not tempt fate*.[14]

Here fate has replaced the tiger, but both images locate the power of deterrence in something other than human intentions. Later I will revisit this passage, which is remarkable for conjoining two con-traries: contingency (the possibility of failure) and necessity (fate). May those who still believe that the reasoning behind the doctrine of mutual assured destruction is too rationalistic agree to wear a dunce's cap.

The reference to fate, which is to say, in philosophical terms, a future in which the things that occur necessarily occur—they cannot, in other words, not occur[15]—does not turn up here by chance. It corresponds to a fundamental theoretical need. If nuclear deterrence has been christened with the name of its failure, MAD, it is because it is uniquely defined by what it is absolutely determined to avoid: nuclear war. To speak of the good, one uses the word *evil* and places a *not* before it. This is the dog that nips to show that it does not bite;[16] the brothers-in-law who mimic being at war with each other, then stop at a critical moment to say that they have made peace;[17] the Christ who accepts sacrifice in order to reveal its deceptive character,[18] and so on. To convey the idea that nuclear war would be the abomination of desolation, one imitates it by means of explicit or implicit threats and makes the failure to carry them out a necessary future, a fate. This, at any rate, is how it seems to me Brodie's words must be interpreted.

Fate has its own specialists, who are called prophets. It is the prophet of doom who interests us, for his purpose, in announcing the imminent occurrence of catastrophe, is to ensure that it will not occur. No one analyzed this apophatic (or negative) metaphysics more clearly than Günther Anders, to whom I referred earlier, the most profound and the most radical theorist of the great catastrophes of the twentieth century. He is less well known than two of his classmates at Marburg, like him students of Heidegger: his future wife Hannah Arendt and his friend Hans Jonas. Anders's relative obscurity is a consequence not only of his own stubbornness but also of the fragmented character of his writings. He abjured great systematic treatises in favor of topical investigations and not infrequently resorted to parables. More than once, he recounted the biblical tale of the flood in a distinctive and original way.[19]

Noah, in his telling, had grown tired of being a prophet of doom whom no one any longer took seriously. And so one day he clothed himself in sackcloth and covered his face with ashes:

Only a man who was mourning [the death of] a beloved child or his wife was allowed to do this. Clothed in the garb of truth, bearer of sorrow, he went back to the city, resolved to turn the curiosity, spitefulness, and superstition of its inhabitants to his advantage. Soon a small crowd of people had gathered around him. They asked him questions. They asked if someone had died, and who the dead person was. Noah replied to them that many had died, and then, to the great amusement of his listeners, said that they themselves were the dead of whom he spoke. When he was asked when this catastrophe had taken place, he replied to them: "Tomorrow." Profiting from their attention and their confusion, Noah drew himself up to his full height and said these words: "The day after tomorrow, the flood will be something that will have been. And when the flood will have been, *everything that is will never have existed.* When the flood will have carried off everything that is, everything that will have been, it will be too late to remember, for there will no longer be anyone alive. And so there will no longer be any difference between the dead and those who mourn them. *If I have come to you in this way, it is in order to reverse time,* to mourn tomorrow's dead today. The day after tomorrow will be too late." With this he went back whence he had come, took off the sackcloth [that he wore], cleaned his face of the ashes that covered it, and went to his workshop. That evening a carpenter knocked on his door and said to him: "Let me help you build an ark, *so that [the prediction of catastrophe] will be false.*" Then a roofer joined them, saying: "It is raining in the mountains, let me help you, *so that it will be false.*"[20]

Mourning deaths that have not yet occurred reverses time in the sense that the effect (mourning) precedes the cause (the deaths). This counterintuitive sequence makes sense only if the deaths being mourned will occur at a determinate date. What makes death bearable for many people is that they liken an unknown end to an indeterminate end, and this indeterminate end to the absence of an end. "Whatever certainty there is in death," La Bruyère remarked, "is mitigated to some extent by that which is uncertain: an indefiniteness in time that has something of the infinite about it."[21]

Anders's aim in this parable, by contrast, is to emphasize that the flood is inevitable, or rather, *will always have been inevitable* once it occurs. It is fated.

The paradox of prophesying doom is as follows. In order to make the prospect of catastrophe credible, it is necessary to maximize the ontological force of its inscription in the future: the sufferings and deaths foretold will inevitably occur. But if the prophet succeeds too well in convincing his listeners of this, the purpose of his performance—to raise their awareness and spur them to action so that the catastrophe does not occur ("Let me help you build an ark, *so that it will be false*")—will have been lost sight of.

What prevents the metaphysics underlying this parable from falling into an archaic and obsolete fatalism is the structure imparted to it by the use of the future perfect tense. Convoluted though it may seem, the future perfect is implicit in much of what one reads today. Consider, for example, this statement from August 2017: "If Mr. Trump's presidency ends in humiliation, future generations may well conclude that it was bound to fail all along."[22] The proposition, when it was asserted, was true if either Trump's presidency would end in humiliation or it was bound to fail all along. The claim being made here was not that Trump's presidency was necessarily doomed, only that if it did turn out to be a failure, it *would have been* destined to be a failure all along. Necessity in this case is retrospective.[23]

Anders's beautiful parable nonetheless remains a poetic expression of abstract ideas, an allegory. In my own work I have tried to give these ideas a formal interpretation within the framework of analytical metaphysics (and analytical theology). I now invite the reader to join me in making a long detour through the metaphysics of time—a rationalistic, rather than a poetic way of thinking about the problem of mutual assured destruction. Once we have reached the end of this journey, everything that we have considered until now will take on a new coloring.

My starting point was an age-old question, whether determinism and free will are compatible, in the modern form given it by David K. Lewis and Robert Stalnaker, each of whom, in his own way, has recast the theory of possible worlds due to Leibniz.[24]

Lewis is concerned to defend what he calls soft determinism, "the doctrine that sometimes one freely does what one is predetermined to do; and that in such a case one is able to act otherwise though past history and the laws of nature determine that one will not act otherwise." He then proceeds to define compatibilism as "the doctrine that soft determinism may be true."[25]

Let us call C the state of the world at t_1. We have

A1: C was the case at t_1

Let S be a subject whose action x at $t_2 > t_1$ is determined by the laws that govern the world according to

A2: If C was the case at t_1, then S does x at t_2

From A1 and A2, by modus ponens,[26] we deduce

A3: S does x at t_2

Can one freely do something even though one is predetermined to do it? In order to answer this question, it will be useful to begin by examining the arguments put forward by those who reject soft determinism. The so-called incompatibilist thesis makes use of the necessity operator, $\Box$. Applied to a proposition p, it states that p is necessary—which is to say that it is true in all possible worlds. In connection more specifically with our problem, let us introduce a necessity operator $\Box_t^S$, where $\Box_t^S(p)$ means: p is true and S is not free at t to perform an act such that, if he were to perform it, p would be false.

The incompatibilist argument can be formulated as follows:

N1: $\Box_{t_2}^S$ (C was the case at t_1)
N2: $\Box_{t_2}^S$ (If C was the case at t_1, then S does x at t_2)

Thus, by modus ponens,

N3: $\Box_{t_2}^S$ (S does x at t_2)[27]

N1 expresses the principle of the fixity of the past. N2 says that the laws that determine the subject's actions remain the same in all the possible worlds that the subject's action could bring about. The conclusion, N3, states that S does actually do x at t_2, but that he does not act freely because it is not in his power to act otherwise.

Can this argument be refuted? Depending on the nature of the problem, there are two possibilities, neither of which has greater a priori legitimacy than the other.

(a) One accepts N1, in which case N2 has to be rejected. The past is fixed, and the subject, who is supposed to be capable of acting otherwise, has the power to invalidate the fixity of the temporal chain that links C to x (the "law"). In order to be very clear about the nature of this power, we must follow Lewis in distinguishing between two versions:

> Strong version: "I am able to break a law."

> Weak version: "I am able to do something such that, if I were to do it, a law would be broken."[28]

Quite obviously it is impossible that *in our world* the subject could act in such a way that the link between C and x would be broken: this would be contrary to hypothesis A2, which of course remains valid. The strong version is therefore eliminated, but not the weak one. As Lewis puts it, the way in which the subject is determined not to do anything other than x is "not the sort of way that counts as inability."[29] The power to break the law is not a causal power. It is a counterfactual power.

(b) Conversely, one accepts N2, in which case N1 has to be rejected. This time the temporal chain A2 is held to be fixed, which is to say true in all possible worlds. To maintain that the subject does x freely, even though his action is predetermined by the past and the laws that govern the world, means having to credit the subject with the power to change the past. Here again we must distinguish between two versions:

> Strong version: "I am able to change the past"—something Lewis rightly calls "utterly incredible."[30]

> Weak version: "I am able to do something such that, if I were to do it, the past would have been different from what it actually was."

The Calvinist theologian and analytic metaphysician Alvin Plantinga, who defends the weak version, has called the ability it supposes a "counterfactual power over the past."[31]

Although, as I say, these two ways of justifying compatibilism have equal legitimacy in principle, philosophers such as Lewis and Stalnaker, perhaps owing to their earlier work in rational choice theory, have focused almost exclusively on the first option, which preserves the fixity of the past.[32] For my part, I have been able to show that the second option makes it possible to elegantly formalize the properties that, as we have seen, characterize the prophecy of doom.

The first thing to be noted is that there are situations in which an agent's counterfactual power over the past causally prevents him from acting in a certain way.[33] Consider, for example, the analysis of promises, a tradition that goes back at least to Hobbes. At t_1, Mary asks Peter to lend her $1,000 and she promises to repay her debt at $t_2 > t_1$. Here we are in a Hobbesian state of nature: there are no state institutions, no judicial system, no rule of law. Agents are guided only by self-interest. It is assumed, furthermore, that if the loan could be arranged, it would be mutually beneficial.

In the conception of time that preserves the fixity of the past, it is clear that the money will not be loaned. Reasoning by backward induction, Peter realizes that Mary at t_2 will not keep her promise: she has no reason to do so. Peter would be a fool to lend her anything.

In the conception of time underlying N2, which assumes a necessary link between past conditions and future action, while sacrificing the fixity of the past, the situation is very different. Suppose that Peter is an omniscient forecaster, capable of anticipating Mary's actions in all possible worlds. If Mary keeps her promise at t_2, Peter will have anticipated it and the mutually beneficial loan would be made. On the other hand, if Mary were to renege on her promise, Peter would have foreseen this as well and would not have agreed to the loan. Here we see the counterfactual power that Mary's future decision has on Peter's decision. And yet if the loan is not made, Mary is not in a position at t_2 to renege on her promise to repay her debt. Hence a contradiction that is immediately resolved: Mary will not renege on her promise if the loan is actually made; the loan will therefore be made and repaid, to the advantage of both Peter and Mary.

This example shows that, in the temporality we are analyzing, it is not true that the future can be anything at all: as Philip K. Dick might have put it, "It's not the future if you stop it."[34] The future must be such that the past it *counterfactually* determines does not *causally* prevent its occurrence. In other words, the future, far from being the outcome of applying the laws of nature to a determinate set of initial conditions (prediction) or a state of affairs that we bring about in accordance with our will (prospective),[35] is the solution (one of the solutions) to an equation in which the unknown x—a future action—appears on both sides of the equal sign in the formula x = F[x], as if it were determining itself.

Following the conventional terminology, let us say that the future is the fixed point of a certain operator F. This operator expresses the causal consequences of a past that itself is determined counterfactually by a future action x. The loop connecting past and future can be represented graphically thus:

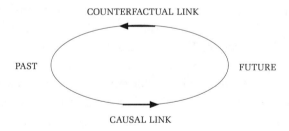

In this conception of time, the future is fixed, which is to say necessary, since it is linked to the past by proposition N2, which states that this link obtains in all possible worlds. The link obtains, however, only if the past is determined, which presupposes that the future is itself determined. In other words, the future is necessary— it has always been necessary—but only once it has been actualized. This is the essential feature that characterizes the metaphysics of the prophecy of doom.

The indeterminacy of the past so long as an action has not taken place, together with the necessity of the future once an action has taken place, define a metaphysics of temporality that I call "projected time." In what follows, in order to prepare the ground for my analysis of nuclear deterrence, I introduce another such metaphysics, which I call "occurring time." It is this version that underlies strategic reasoning in its various forms, whether it informs the work of economists, game theorists, planners, engineers, designers, or military strategists. Occurring time rests on a quite singular conception of free will, known as the belief/desire model, which regards an agent's actions as "pulled" by a set of beliefs and desires rather than "pushed" by a particular determinism. The most familiar graphical representation of this model today is the decision tree. At every node of the tree an agent has a choice between several possible future courses of action. When he chooses among them, he takes the past to be fixed, which is to say counterfactually—and not only causally—independent of his choosing. This temporality, characterized by a fixed past and an open future, stands sharply in contrast with the metaphysics of projected time.

If metaphysics, as it is usually said, is the branch of philosophy that explores the fundamental nature of reality, the question arises how we are to account for the plurality of possible metaphysics. In the fourth century BCE, a member of the Megarian School named Diodorus Cronus devised an axiomatic system—a set of propositions and rules of inference held to be self-evidently true or truth-preserving—with the purpose of showing that the actual world is the only possible world and that the future is predetermined. The three axioms are the following:

1. Every true proposition about the past is necessarily true (i.e., the past is fixed).

2. The impossible cannot be deduced from the possible (just as, in logic, the false cannot be deduced from the true).

3. Something that neither is nor will be is possible (i.e., there is a possible that neither is presently true nor will be true).

Diodorus demonstrated that these propositions are incompatible. At least one of them is therefore false. The third proposition seems incontestable to most philosophers today. If, however, they follow Diodorus in holding that (1) and (2) are self-evident, then they must give up (3). They must, in other words, consider an event that occurs neither in the present nor the future to be an impossible event.

Jules Vuillemin, one of the greatest French philosophers of the twentieth century, wrote a fascinating history of Western metaphysics on the basis of which axiom or axioms Diodorus's successors decided to drop in order to eliminate the incompatibility.[36] Aristotle rejected the necessitarianism of the Megarian School, proposing instead a theory of future contingents—statements concerning future events, states, or actions that are neither impossible nor inevitable—that rests on the indeterminacy of the future.[37] These statements, he held, cannot be said to be true or false before the event, state, or action occurs. Aristotle could not imagine that necessity and indeterminacy could be combined in the manner I am about to suggest.

The origin of the multiplicity of metaphysics is to be found in Diodorus's incompatibility theorem. A comparison with the history of geometry comes to mind. Once it was finally demonstrated that Euclid's fifth axiom, the so-called parallel axiom, could not be derived from the first four, constructing a geometry in which this axiom does not hold became conceivable. From this followed the concept of a Riemannian manifold, which proved to be extremely useful to Einstein in elaborating the theory of general relativity. As the great mathematician Henri Poincaré asked, "What, then, are we to think of the question: Is Euclidean geometry true? [The question] has no meaning. . . . One geometry cannot be more true than another; it can only be more convenient."[38] By the same token, there is no point asking whether projected time is truer than occurring time. What matters is whether one is more useful than the other.

It all depends on the kind of problem one is dealing with. Both projected time and occurring time are ways of finding a way out from the impasse Diodorus identified. Projected time rejects axioms (1) and (3); occurring time accepts each of these and rejects (2).[39] In my work on the philosophy of catastrophe[40]—including the possibility of a nuclear conflict—I have shown that projected time makes it possible to avoid many of the paradoxes that cripple strategic thinking, which is to say the metaphysics of occurring time, when it tries to think about a looming catastrophe whose date is unknown. Projected time implies a very special attitude toward the future—neither complacency nor fatalism. Complacency considers that catastrophe, though possible, is not inevitable: the future is undecided. Fatalism considers catastrophe to be inevitable. By granting agents the counterfactual power to act on the past, which is to say on the conditions that determine their behavior, projected time helps them steer a safe course between the devil of doomsaying and the deep blue sea of smug optimism.

Our zeitgeist favors smug optimism, as we have already seen. We would do well to recall, then, that the experience of projected time has inspired the human imagination since the dawn of history. It is intimately linked to the religious apprehension of the world. In all traditional societies there are people called prophets whose role is to transmit and interpret the divinity's will. Prophets in general, and the Biblical prophet (*nabi*) in particular, must solve a fixed-point problem. They must predict a future that the people to whom they speak will regard as inalterable, while taking into account the fact that this future will be caused in part by the prophecy that has been publicly announced.[41] From this, there results a highly paradoxical combination of fatalism and voluntarism: fatalism on the side of the people, who take the word of the prophet to be the word of God, and voluntarism (at least partially) on the side of the prophet, who knows that his words have a causal impact on the future. Revolutionary prophecy, particularly in the form it came to acquire in Marxist doctrine, has preserved this dual quality. As the German philosopher Hans Jonas[42] remarked, dialectical materialism is "a most peculiar mixture of colossal responsibility for the future with deterministic release from responsibility."[43]

The metaphysics of projected time enables us to extend the notion of prophecy to our secular age and substitute for the obscure dialectic between voluntarism and fatalism a rigorous and non-paradoxical alternative. For the modern prophet, especially the prophet of doom, it is necessary to locate the fixed point of the loop between past and future, the point where anticipation of the future by the past and causal production of the future by the past coincide. In this sense, prophets are legion in modern democratic societies based on science and technology. The experience of projected time is facilitated, encouraged, organized, and indeed imposed by the many more or less authoritative forecasts of the more or less near future that are commonplace in today's world: the next day's traffic on the highway, the results of the upcoming elections,[44] the rates of inflation and growth for the coming year, changes in the level of greenhouse-gas emissions, and so on. Futurists and other prognosticators know perfectly well, as we do, that the future they announce to us as though it were written in the stars is in fact, at least partially, a future of our own making. Because we do not allow ourselves to be troubled by what some would regard as a philosophical scandal, nothing prevents us from experiencing projected time.

Nuclear Deterrence in Projected Time

It is now possible to rigorously show that the implicit metaphysics of nuclear deterrence in its existential form is projected time. This is a metaphysics that, by definition, holds the future to be necessary. The renunciation of strategy, the appeal to destiny, the apparent fatalism—all these things point in the same direction.

In occurring time, the questions that have been raised by critics of mutual assured destruction, and especially the doubts about the credibility of this threat, are interpreted in a straightforward manner. The argument against the credibility of nuclear deterrence in its MAD form is a strategic one. Reasoning by backward induction,[45] one asks what an agent who threatens an escalation of violence would do if its bluff were to be called by a first strike. If the agent is rational in the sense assumed by game theory, it will prefer to yield rather than be annihilated.[46] In that case the potential aggressor would not have been deterred, for it could launch an attack with impunity. The question arises, then, whether projected time provides a basis for demonstrating the effectiveness and rationality of nuclear deterrence by resolving the prudential paradox on the formal level.

The answer would appear to be no. If the future is necessary, then no form of deterrence will work. Let us suppose that deterrence does work and the event that is to be prevented does not take place. The event is therefore impossible.[47] Therefore there is nothing to protect oneself against. Let us unpack this argument as it applies to the case of nuclear deterrence:

1. If nuclear deterrence works, the threat of escalating violence to its ultimate point, mutual annihilation, is not carried out.

2. If an escalation to extremes does not take place, then it is impossible.

3. If it is impossible, then nuclear deterrence does not work, because the threat has no reality.

4. It follows from this that if nuclear deterrence works, then it does not work.

5. Therefore nuclear deterrence does not work.

This reasoning provides a solid foundation for the second argument put forward by the critics of MAD. What they call the self-defeating or self-stultifying character of successful deterrence is simply another way of describing the reductio ad absurdum expressed by propositions (4) and (5).

The metaphysics of projected time appears, then, to be no more successful in demonstrating the effectiveness and rationality of nuclear deterrence than occurring time. There is a way to make it successful, however. This consists in taking seriously Bernard Brodie's remark about fate, which I quoted earlier and recall once more:

It is the curious paradox of our time that one of the foremost factors making deterrence really work and work well is the lurking fear that in some massive confrontation crisis it may fail. Under these circumstances *one does not tempt fate.*

It will shortly become clear that the paradoxes besetting the theory of deterrence can in fact readily be resolved in projected time.

Nuclear Deterrence and the Indeterminacy of the Future

The idea that uncertainty can be manipulated strategically to solve the problem of credibility is by no means new. The conviction that minimally rational agents will not carry out their threat to continue down the road leading to mutual assured destruction all the way to the end gave rise more than fifty years ago to the suspicion, formalized by Thomas Schelling and popularized by Richard Nixon, that it may be rational to pretend to be irrational. The limits of Nixon's Madman Theory were rapidly reached, as we have seen.

With Brodie, however, we are no longer talking about strategy. The dual reference to fate and to the possibility of failure or of an accident[48] brings us into a completely different world. The idea that fate comes to pass as the result of an accident is as old as the most ancient myths. One thinks of Oedipus. The Delphic oracle proclaimed that he would commit parricide and incest. Its prophecy proved to be true, but only on account of a random encounter with an irascible old man who barred his way. One thinks also of the modern tragedy recounted by Albert Camus in *The Stranger*. The hero of this sad tale, Meursault, is doomed from the very first line to end up on the scaffold. And yet for this actually to be his destiny, it was necessary for him, in the middle of the book, to commit a senseless murder under the blazing midday sun, an inexplicable act that was pure contingency. The merger of fate and accident is a theme common to many religious traditions as well. The Romans worshipped a goddess who personified both luck (good or bad) and fate—or, to use the language of modal logic, contingency and necessity. Her name was Fortuna.

Once again the metaphysics of projected time enables us to interpret these intuitions in a precise and formalizable way. The key is a concept that I have not yet introduced: the uncertainty of the future in projected time.

The uncertainty of the future in occurring time may be formalized using the usual tools of decision theory, elaborated in the first instance by the mathematical statistician Leonard Savage, which assumes the future to be uncertain but probabilizable.[49] Let us come back to the Madman Theory. A power confronted with insane behavior on the part of a foreign leader must ask itself whether the folly is feigned, in which case it is probable that he will flinch if his bluff is called, or whether he really is mad, in which case he may not hesitate to escalate hostilities to the point of mutual destruction if attacked. A rational agent is supposed to ascribe a small (hopefully, very small) subjective probability epsilon to the latter possibility and the complement $1 - \varepsilon$ to the former. The way in which the agent arrives at a decision is left up to him. He may consider that the Savage criterion for maximizing expected utility has no meaning in the case of an extreme event where the consequences are enormous and epsilon exceedingly small.[50] One thing is assured in any case: the two possibilities to be considered constitute a non-overlapping partition of the set of possible worlds—a so-called exclusive disjunction: one or the other, not both.

In projected time, uncertainty takes on a radically different form. There are no alternative possible futures since the future is necessary. Instead of exclusive disjunction, there is a *superposition of states*. Both the escalation to extremes and its absence are part of a fixed future: it is because the former figures in it that deterrence has a chance to work; it is because the latter figures in it that the adversaries are not bound to destroy each other. Only the future, when it comes to pass, will tell.

What distinguishes the two forms of uncertainty is this. In occurring time, epsilon, the probability of the catastrophic scenario, can be equal to zero without that leading to a contradiction. In projected time, where epsilon designates the relative weight of this scenario in the superposition of states, it is essential that epsilon remain strictly positive.[51] If it were equal to zero, escalation to extremes would be absent from the future and therefore impossible, and deterrence would fail—not in the sense that a nuclear apocalypse would be avoided (crisis stability), but in the sense that a potential attacker would not be deterred (noncrisis stability). Superposition of states and strict positivity of epsilon are kindred concepts.

I arrived at the concept of superposition of states by a line of reasoning that owes nothing to quantum theory. Even so, there are unmistakable affinities, at the very least, between the metaphysics of projected time and some of the basic concepts of quantum mechanics.[52] This is why I have elected to call the kind of uncertainty proper to projected time indeterminacy—the correct translation of the German word *Unbestimmtheit*, which Heisenberg used to name his famous *Unbestimmtheitsrelation*, unfortunately translated in respect of both of its elements as the "uncertainty principle."

We now arrive at a preliminary conclusion: what has allowed nuclear deterrence to work until now, and may allow it to go on working, is *the indeterminacy of the future in a conception of time that makes the future necessary.*[53]

On Vanishingly Small Magnitudes

The quantitative consequences of a nuclear war would be immensely great: not hundreds of thousands of deaths, as at the beginning of the atomic era, but hundreds of millions. These numbers are so far beyond our power to imagine that they arouse no emotion. In the minds of many people they are vastly reduced by the unlikelihood of such a thing happening: unconsciously multiplying the almost infinitely large magnitude of the damage that would be caused by the infinitely small magnitude of its probability, they are easily reassured. From the point of view of a mathematician, however, this operation produces only indeterminacy.

The British philosopher Derek Parfit, in one of the most original works of consequentialist ethics of the twentieth century, *Reasons and Persons*, posed the following question: There exist actions or facts that have an extremely low probability of producing a considerable effect; because they are insignificant, can a rational moral calculus consider them to be null? Parfit treats this problem in the third chapter of his book ("Five Mistakes in Moral Mathematics"), where he also considers a question that may be thought of as the dual[54] of the first: There exist actions or facts that produce imperceptible effects but that affect a very large number of persons; because these effects are imperceptible, ought they be disregarded?[55]

I will begin by taking up the second question, which I examined in the course of my work on the health consequences of the nuclear accident that occurred at Chernobyl on 26 April 1986.[56] This made it necessary to think about the relation between the two aspects of nuclear energy: the civil sector, on the one hand, which is dedicated to the cause of peace and prosperity,[57] and the military sector, on the other, which cannot hide the fact that it is an instrument of death.

In 2005, nineteen years after the catastrophe, the report of the Chernobyl Forum, a multiagency organ of the United Nations, was made public. According to the accompanying press release, "a total of up to 4,000 people could eventually die of radiation exposure from the Chernobyl Nuclear Power Plant (NPP) accident nearly twenty years ago, an international team of more than 100 scientists has concluded."[58] So small a figure is bound to come as a surprise, especially if it is compared with the statement made in 2000 by the secretary-general of the United Nations, Kofi Annan, referring to the "seven million victims of Chernobyl," three million of them children requiring ongoing medical treatment.[59] Thus Annan's own agencies disavowed his words five years later.

More than thirty years have now passed since the catastrophe, and the gap between these two estimates has not narrowed. Epistemologically, this is truly a scandalous state of affairs. Accusing those who administer and monitor the nuclear industry of intellectual dishonesty does not amount to a satisfactory explanation. There is a deeper reason, I believe, which has to do with two fundamentally opposed attitudes toward what is, at bottom, a philosophical problem.

Three methods are available for estimating the effects on human health of a nuclear catastrophe: direct observation, epidemiological investigation, and modeling. The radiation exposure of the first responders to the accident was so great that their deaths can be attributed to it with complete certainty. For all those who were exposed to moderate or low doses of radiation at the moment of the accident and afterward, the situation is much more complicated. In principle, epidemiological analysis can retrospectively estimate the excess of malignant illnesses in a population exposed to radiation over the rate that would normally be expected. This analysis was not properly performed in the case of Chernobyl for two reasons. On the one hand, the most affected populations—the liquidators[60] and the persons living closest to the plant who had to be evacuated—were dispersed throughout the Soviet Union, and no systematic follow-up study was able to be made. On the other hand, for the millions of persons who were exposed to low amounts of radiation, epidemiological analysis could have detected a possible increase (small, indeed very small) in rates of mortality from leukemia or cancer only at an exorbitant cost in funds and resources that the Soviet Union, then on the verge of disintegration, was incapable of mobilizing. Modeling was therefore substituted for epidemiological investigation.

The model used by the International Commission on Radiological Protection (ICRP) assumes that the effect on morbidity and mortality is proportional to the amount of radiation exposure, even where this amount is very small. In other words, there exists no radiation threshold below which the postulated effect is nil. The ICRP justified this assumption on prudential grounds: it overestimated the real effect since a positive threshold, which many experts believe exists, renders the effect nonexistent for the smallest amounts. The physicist Georges Charpak, a Nobel laureate, has given the modeling assumption a scientific basis, however, by means of the following argument. The effects of radioactivity on cellular metabolism are similar to the spontaneous accidents that cause the "natural" cancers from which 20 percent of a given population die; nothing distinguishes a radiation-induced cancer from an ordinary cancer. Since the effect of low levels of radiation is marginal by comparison with other causes of cancer, an increase in the rate of cancer due to radiation can reasonably be assumed to be proportional to the amount of radiation exposure, even where it is very small. Indeed, this is the very basis of the differential calculus.[61]

The proportional model has a very important implication: the number of deaths due to radiation in a given population is a function only of the overall amount of radiation to which it is exposed, independently therefore of its distribution in time and space. An overall amount to which a small part of the population is exposed for a very brief period of time will have the same quantitative effect as the same overall amount affecting the entire population for a very long period of time.

On reading the report of the Chernobyl Forum more carefully, one discovers that the 4,000 announced deaths were calculated by applying the proportional model only to a small part of the total population exposed to the radiation released by the accident: barely 600,000 persons, or about 200,000 liquidators, 120,000 evacuated persons, and 280,000 others living in the most contaminated areas. The official estimate has nothing to say about the millions of other persons affected by the radiation, which everyone understood to mean that the catastrophe was not responsible for any deaths among them. When the proportional model is applied to these other persons as well, if only for reasons of internal consistency, one finds, as Charpak did, that the nuclear accident at Chernobyl will have caused the deaths of tens of thousands. Let there be no misunderstanding: it may be that the proportional model, which postulates the absence of a threshold below which the effects on health and mortality are nil, is inaccurate and considerably overestimates the number of deaths; what is unacceptable is to say that the model has been applied to the whole of a population when in fact it has been applied only to a small part—as if, having regretted accepting a high calculation, one sought to atone for the misjudgment by employing the model only on a very partial basis.

When radioactive exposure is very spread out in time and distributed over a vast population, as in the case of Chernobyl, it is impossible to say that the death of any particular person from a cancer or leukemia was caused by the accident that occurred there. The most that we can say is that the a priori probability of a person's dying from a cancer or leukemia was very slightly increased by Chernobyl. The tens of thousands of deaths that will have been caused by the nuclear catastrophe therefore cannot be named, that is, cannot be individually assigned. The official position concludes from this that they do not exist.

The crucial problem is to determine the physical meaning of the number that is obtained by multiplying a very large magnitude, N—which stands for the affected population—by a very small number, ε—which stands for the increase in the probability of dying from a cancer or leukemia as a result of Chernobyl. This product, Nε, therefore represents some number of deaths. But it is impossible to isolate a set of Nε individuals of whom it may be said that these are the persons who died as a result of Chernobyl. From there it was but a small step for the Chernobyl Forum to consider ε, and therefore Nε as well, to be equal to zero. In this way the set of persons who died as a result of Chernobyl becomes an empty set. We can and must refuse to accept this judgment. But we then have to answer the question of what reality is to be attributed to these Nε deaths.

This problem is a paradox known since antiquity as the paradox of the heap.[62] One stone does not amount to a heap; adding a stone to a set of stones that do not amount to a heap does not transform it into a heap; and yet a heap of stones is nothing more than a certain number of stones placed on top of one another. Or, if you like, a man who has only a few hairs on his head is bald; grafting one more hair onto his skull does not make him non-bald; and yet a non-bald person is simply someone who has a certain number of hairs on his head. Today, with the help of a branch of mathematics known as non-standard arithmetic, it is possible to clear up this paradox.

Let ε be a very small number. It is not a variable; it is a number belonging to the set of real positive numbers. This number —itself positive, which is to say non-zero—is said to be vanishingly small.[63] Since it is greater than zero, there exists a whole number N—an integer—such that the product Nε is a non-vanishing real number A. And yet the vanishingly small character of epsilon means that the result of adding it to a real number X is indiscernible from X, and therefore identical to X, in accordance with Leibniz's principle of the identity of indiscernibles.[64]

X + ε is identical to X, even though ε is a positive number, greater than zero: this is the paradox of the heap. The mathematician John Allen Paulos tells an apocryphal story that illustrates this apparently extraordinary property. A guide at the Museum of Natural

History in New York is explaining to a group of visitors that the majestic tyrannosaur enthroned in the middle of the hall is seventy million and six years old. "What?" a little girl asks. "Seventy million and six years? Are you sure?" "Oh, I'm quite sure," replies the guide. "When I started work here I was told that it was seventy million years old. And that was six years ago."[65]

A T. rex that is seventy million and six years old is identical to a T. rex that is seventy million years old. Given this identity between X and X + ε, the paradox of the bald man is easily explained. Let us assume that having X hairs makes a man bald but that having X + A hairs makes him non-bald, where A = Nε. Decomposing A into N times ε, we see that X, the sign of being bald, never drops out, on account of the identity between X and X + ε. Nevertheless we have succeeded in giving a physical meaning to the product Nε, which represents the transitional state from baldness to non-baldness.

Paulos was led to formulate this parable in the wake of the 2000 presidential election, when it seemed impossible to separate the vote counts of the two candidates, Al Gore and George W. Bush, despite many recounts. Indeed, there is no better illustration of the paradox of the heap than the case of national elections. Two candidates vie with each other for our votes, or a referendum offers us the choice between two options. Except in the extremely improbable case (perhaps a chance of one in a billion) where all the other votes cast, apart from one's own, are equally divided between the two options, it is incontestable that any individual vote will have had no effect whatever on the outcome. To the question, Would the final result have been different if I had voted otherwise than I did (or even if I hadn't voted)?, each member of the electorate must admit that the answer is no. And yet the result of the vote is supposed to follow immediately from the counting of individual votes.

This paradox is readily cleared up as well. We have only to appeal to a symbolic way of thinking, the way of thinking that we spontaneously adopt in situations such as this. The result of such votes, even when they are close—indeed, especially when they are close—we interpret as a carefully considered choice made by a collective subject: the people, the electorate, and so on. As a matter of rationality, in the narrow sense assumed by decision theorists, this collective subject is a pure fiction. Yet appeal to a collective subject resolves the moral paradox in respect of responsibility. By parity of reasoning, the catastrophe of Chernobyl was responsible for tens of thousands of deaths, without taking into account the many illnesses that have made life painful for millions of people.

Now that we have familiarized ourselves with vanishingly small magnitudes, it is time to come back to Parfit's first question, concerning actions or facts having an extremely small probability of producing a considerable effect. Here N measures the effect, and ε the vanishingly small probability.

Daniel Ellsberg, in *The Doomsday Machine*, analyzes a perfectly exemplary case, where N represents the disappearance of humanity and all life on earth, microbes included. This is the risk that the scientists working on the Manhattan Project believed they were taking when they exploded the first atomic bomb on 16 July 1945 in the New Mexico desert. Some of the best physicists in the world considered it to be very unlikely, but not impossible, that this explosion would ignite the earth's atmosphere together with the hydrogen in the oceans and swallow up the entire planet in fire. Enrico Fermi was the most pessimistic member of Robert Oppenheimer's team, whereas Hans Bethe thought that atmospheric ignition was an absolute impossibility. Arthur Compton, who was in charge of the project, decided that if calculation showed that the chances were more than three in a million (or a probability of 0.000003) that the earth would be vaporized by the explosion, he would not proceed further. Calculation proved the chances to be slightly less, and the project continued.[66]

What exactly did the threshold insisted on by Compton amount to? Ellsberg's answer is significant for its apparent imprecision: something "small, very small . . . but not zero."[67] This means that the threshold is neither a definite magnitude nor a variable, but an epsilon in the sense already indicated: a number belonging to the set of real numbers such that its addition to any real number has no discernible effect. Treated as a probability, its multiplication by N, an infinitely large number—and what could be greater for human beings than the disappearance of their kind?—leads to the very question we are now considering.

Ellsberg recounts the dread during the hours, as well as the minutes and seconds, prior to the start of the chain reaction. His account is worthy of the best suspense films. Fermi, the evening before, was taking bets at fixed odds on two events: the incineration of the whole of New Mexico and of the entire world. Was he joking in order to relieve the tension? Many of the scientists present did not think so. During the countdown, a young physicist was responsible for deciding whether to push a button that would abort the process; in the last seconds, his hand trembling, he could not resist the temptation to ask Oppenheimer for permission to abort. The explosion released a light brighter than a thousand suns. James Conant, the president of Harvard, later recalled that for a moment he believed that the fears Fermi had aroused, which he and others had not taken seriously, had been realized. He thought that the whole world had gone up in flames.[68]

Compton, in a memoir written ten years later, asked himself: "Was there really any chance than an atomic bomb would trigger the explosion of the nitrogen in the atmosphere or of the hydrogen in the ocean? This would be the ultimate catastrophe. *Better to accept the slavery of the Nazis than to run a chance of drawing the final curtain on mankind!*"[69] Ellsberg, noting that the Nazis were just then in the process of implementing the "final solution," asks whether the infinitesimal risk of causing the extinction of humankind could have really been considered more grave than the certainty of being enslaved by the Nazis. Some scientists at the time believed that it was. For them, the product εN was the worst abomination imaginable. But this did not prevent them from helping to detonate the first atomic bomb in human history. On 16 July 1945 at 5:29 a.m. at Alamogordo, New Mexico, United States of America.

In his work as a rational choice theorist, Ellsberg is known for formulating a paradox that, along with an earlier one due to Maurice Allais,[70] undermined the axioms on which Savage had built his method for maximizing expected utility. Ellsberg is interested today[71] in studying the ethical dimension of a decision to explode a nuclear warhead under uncertainty (or, as I should say, indeterminacy) no less radical than that which obtained in 1945. His view is that it is necessary to rely on a lexicographical (or lexical) ordering principle, which is to say an order of priorities in which a criterion of judgment considered to be superior to another has infinite weight by comparison with it: no sacrifice in respect of the first criterion can be compensated by a more complete satisfaction of the second.[72] John Rawls's theory of justice made this method of classification both famous and controversial for its argument that depriving a person of basic liberties, however minimally, cannot be justified on the ground that doing so would contribute to greater economic justice. Well-being cannot be purchased at the cost of slavery.[73] Similarly, Ellsberg argues, an infinite weight ought to have been assigned in 1945 to minimizing the probability of a nuclear war. He gives another example. Let us suppose that the member states of NATO, during the Cold War, had launched a first nuclear strike against the Soviet Union, killing six hundred million people, in order to prevent the Soviet Union from extending its control over the whole of Europe. Would the game have been worth the candle? Evidently NATO thought so. Ellsberg's criterion of justice rejects such a conclusion.

The criterion of minimizing the probability of nuclear war and the ensuing apocalypse is not sufficiently precise for our purposes. The options for achieving this result need to be specified. Let us take as our point of departure a slightly different question, which Ellsberg poses in his book: with regard to the problems with which we are concerned, at what level of risk must we consider the risk to be indefensibly great and therefore not to be taken in any case? This means deciding, in order of increasingly stringent conditions, whether we are to be satisfied if

1. the probability ε of C, the potential catastrophe, is vanishingly small, which is to say infinitesimal but positive;

2. ε is zero;

3. C will not happen;

4. C is impossible.

Most of those who played leading roles in the drama of 16 July 1945 thought that (1) was in principle insufficient and that the condition expressed by (2) needed to be satisfied. Nevertheless, with the exception of Bethe, who was inalterably convinced of the *physical* impossibility of igniting the atmosphere, they were content with an approximation, which is to say that, as a practical matter, like Compton, they considered (1) to be sufficient. It is widely believed that there is no such thing as zero risk—a foolish piece of popular wisdom, foolish because it ignores fundamental distinctions.

Looking at the matter a bit more closely, we can see that (2) is not sufficient, because what we want to be assured of is (3) and because (2) does not guarantee (3). Many events can occur despite their a priori probability being nil.[74] On reaching stage (3), one may be tempted to go still further, for even if it is true that catastrophe will not occur, it is nonetheless true that it *could* occur—a possibility that we examined earlier in connection with two historical cases: Reagan's refusal to abandon the Star Wars project at Reykjavik in October 1986 and Chirac's resumption of French nuclear tests in the Pacific during the summer of 1995.

This, quite obviously, supposes that (3) does not imply (4), which is to say that a possible event might never occur. This is Diodorus's third axiom. If it is rejected, we then find ourselves in the metaphysics of projected time, which I have shown is compatible, more than any other, with the logic of nuclear deterrence in its existential form.

Thus we are led, by successive stages of increasing ethical exigency, to state the question posed by Ellsberg in connection with nuclear deterrence (at what level of risk must we consider the risk to be intolerable?) more precisely by placing it in a conception of time that holds the future to be necessary.

At once one runs up against the paradox of self-stultification, which we have studied in some detail. If it is required that the escalation to extremes that a nuclear war, limited to begin with, is bound to generate never occurs, then nuclear war must be made impossible; but if it is impossible, it has no deterrent effect since it has no reality. Resorting like Bernard Brodie to the metaphor of destiny, one averts the prospect of catastrophe by regarding it as fated, but if it is averted, then plainly it was not fated after all. The cataclysmic future that one succeeds in preventing cannot be a necessary future since it does not occur.

Thus one is naturally led to introduce a vanishingly small epsilon, not as the *possibility* of a nuclear war but in superposition with the success of deterrence. This epsilon makes it possible to get around the obstacle of successful deterrence that is self-stultifying by making the escalation to extremes a part of the future, thereby allowing this escalation to have a deterrent effect, but at the price of making it possible also that deterrence will fail.

Violence in Conflict with Itself

Steven P. Lee, whose 1996 book identified the many paradoxes I have tried to resolve in the present chapter, published a no less remarkable article eight years later titled "What's Living and What's Dead in Nuclear Ethics?"[75] Not the least of the merits of the argument he advances is that it turns inside out what most military strategists and academic theorists take for granted—that MAD, this aggravated form of nuclear deterrence that bears the name of its failure, mutual assured destruction,[76] is a thing of the past, a barbarity that would best be forgotten. Lee maintains, quite to the contrary, that with the advent of the atomic bomb, humanity lost its innocence, and we are now forever more caught in the toils of the moral paradox embodied by MAD. Nothing will deliver us from it, neither the course of geopolitics nor the development of new technologies, whether these bear upon offensive weapons or launch vehicles or antimissile systems, not even a denuclearization of the world. MAD has not always existed, of course. It was brought into the world during the Cold War—we have examined the difficult circumstances of its birth—but now it hovers over us like a Platonic form or the grotesque and baleful images of the Japanese pop artist Takashi Murakami evoking Hiroshima, and it will be with us so long as we have not blown up the planet.

When Lee's article was published in 2004, the Soviet Union was no more, and Russia was no longer the enemy of the United States, which now appeared to be the sole superpower. What difference did that make to the global nuclear situation from the moral point of view? It may be worth recalling once more that, to begin with, MAD was neither a doctrine nor a strategy. It was a military state of affairs in which each of the rival nuclear powers had the capacity to destroy the other's society, even after a crippling first strike, since this did not nullify the capacity of either one to respond. The power of nuclear weapons by itself made such a situation possible, for the first time in human history. This very power renders all attempts at defense futile and any thought of a preemptive attack mad. There remains only deterrence. That Russia and the United States were no longer enemies is a purely contingent fact—the proof is that this ceased to be the case on February 24, 2022, with Putin's invasion of Ukraine. MAD is capable of assuming another strategic configuration at any moment.

It is the abiding possibility of mutual assured destruction, and not its incarnation in a particular historical circumstance, that poses the moral paradox. This paradox, it will be recalled, places ethics in contradiction with itself. On the one hand, deterrence appears to be the only means of avoiding a nuclear war and mutual destruction. Consequentialism therefore not only approves it but considers it to be a moral obligation. On the other hand, deterrence rests on threats, whether they are expressed in words or conveyed by the weapons themselves (existential deterrence), which, if they were to be transformed into actions, would constitute a supreme evil. Both the doctrine of just war and deontological ethics, however, are concerned with intentions no less than actions. The tension between these two attitudes is an ineliminable fact of our nuclear condition, whether the direst consequences come to pass or remain merely potential.

There are two ways in which a particular incarnation of MAD could be ended: on the one hand, an agreement not to settle differences by armed conflict, though this could not be expected to last indefinitely; on the other, the abolition of nuclear weapons, though this, according to Lee at least (the question is much disputed),[77] would have the effect only of relocating the moral paradox. Nuclear weapons can be gotten rid of, but the means of making them cannot be unlearned. In a situation of "global zero,"[78] which is to say the complete elimination of nuclear weapons, every nation threatens its enemies with rearming before they do. From this, as we saw earlier, there results what Jonathan Schell calls a regime of weaponless deterrence. If in fact, as Lee claims to show, this regime is less stable than that of armed deterrence, consequentialism would insist on the latter; deontology would insist on the former. Global denuclearization would therefore do nothing to dispel the moral paradox.

I have said more than once that MAD is an aggravated version of nuclear deterrence. I should say exactly why I believe this to be so. When competition takes the form of a game of chicken, which is to say a zero-sum game, played by two nations at the edge of the abyss, where little is at stake by comparison with the plunge of humanity into the downward spiral of global destruction, there is nonetheless something that the adversaries find worth their while to contest: influence over a region, possession of a territory, the prestige that comes from conquest, and so on.[79] It is therefore because they want the same thing that the rivals risk toppling over into the abyss, but it is also because they still find reasons to quarrel that they do not fall into it so easily. The situation under MAD is completely different. There is no longer anything for the rivals to contest. MAD is the ultimate stage of violence, where the only thing that matters is protecting oneself against the lethal blows of the other. But how does one protect oneself? By recourse to the very same violence.

Earlier, drawing on the anthropology of violence and the sacred developed by René Girard, I proposed a solution to the prudential paradox that relies on his great insight—namely, that human violence is capable of self-regulation and self-transcendence: violence is able to put itself outside itself in the form of the principal institutions of society, among them religion, government, the economy, and war, and in this way to hold itself in check.[80] There is no better framework for thinking about the ultimate stage of violence represented by MAD, in which violence is concerned with nothing but itself. From this anthropological perspective, I believe, it becomes possible to understand Lee's claim that we will not be able to deliver ourselves from the curse of mutual assured destruction, finding extreme violence both our only means of protection (the consequentialist argument) and the reason for our condemnation (nothing can justify killing hundreds of millions of people, or forming the intention to do so, not even our willingness to shift responsibility for this unspeakable objective onto mechanisms we have voluntarily given up the power to control).

As a philosopher working in the analytic tradition, Lee was not interested in investigating the anthropological dimension of the problem and restricted his attention to the moral paradox. But here again it seems to me that he did not go far enough, having failed to resolve the prudential paradox. My aim, in these concluding pages, is to fill this gap. In order to do that, it will be necessary to come back to rational metaphysics—the very discipline that made it possible to propose a new solution to the vexed problem of accounting for the effectiveness and rationality of nuclear deterrence.

Recall the preliminary conclusion we arrived at earlier in this chapter: what has allowed nuclear deterrence to work until now, and may allow it to go on working, is the indeterminacy of the future in a conception of time that makes the future necessary. I have inevitably been led by the nature of my approach to think of this indeterminacy in terms of a superposition of states. As long as the future has not been actualized, it must be conceived as including both the catastrophic event and its non-occurrence—not as disjunctive possibilities, but as a conjunction of states of which one or the other will prove a posteriori to have been necessary once the present has selected it.[81]

In the work of Günther Anders, whose radicalism I have noted more than once, one finds a philosophy of the future not so very far removed from the one I have been sketching here. Anders recognized that on 6 August 1945, human history had entered into a new phase, its last. Or, rather, that the sixth day of August was only a rehearsal for the ninth—what he called the "Nagasaki syndrome." The atomic bombing of a civilian population, once it had occurred for the first time, once it had made the unthinkable real, inevitably invited more atrocities, in the same way that an earthquake is inevitably followed by a series of aftershocks. History, Anders said, became obsolete that day. Now that humanity was capable of destroying itself, nothing could cause it to lose this "negative all-powerfulness," not even a general disarmament, not even a total denuclearization of the world's arsenals. Apocalypse having been inscribed in our future as fate, henceforth the best we can do is to indefinitely postpone the final moment. We are now living under a suspended sentence, as it were, a stay of execution. In August 1945, humanity entered into an era of reprieve (*die Frist*), the "second death" of all that had existed: since the meaning of the past depends on our future actions, it follows from the obsolescence of the future, from its programmed end, not that the past no longer has any meaning but that it never had one. This deadline, which is to say the time that remains to us before the apocalypse, is indeterminate.[82] What Anders's view and mine have in common is that each of us—by joining necessity and contingency, fatalism and indeterminacy in novel ways—elaborates a conception of the future that goes beyond the traditional categories of modal logic.

Finally, we need to work out the implications of what we have learned in connection with vanishingly small magnitudes. In the superposition of catastrophe and non-catastrophe that obtains in the future, the solution to the prudential paradox implies that the weight assigned to catastrophe is vanishingly small.[83] To say that it is vanishingly small does not mean that it is zero: the approximation with which physicists are often satisfied is inadmissible in metaphysics. For it is the strict positivity of epsilon that allows catastrophe to have a secure place in the future.[84] This is precisely what Lee misses when he claims that MAD is a permanent condition. Limiting himself to the ethics of intentions, he fails to see that the solution to the prudential paradox requires that the catastrophe nuclear war would bring about not be confined to the stage of threats but that it belong wholly to the reality of the future. The tension within ethics between consequentialism and ordinary morality, between

violence as the remedy for violence and the horror of nuclear violence, is exacerbated to the breaking point.

The time has come to sum up. Yes, it is indeed possible to supply
rational foundations for the effectiveness of nuclear deterrence.
And this conclusion is terrifying.[85]

Appendix

Humanity is more than ever the author of its own fall because it has become able to destroy its world. With respect to Christianity, this is not just an ordinary moral condemnation, but an unavoidable anthropological observation. Therefore we have to wake up our sleeping consciences. Seeking to comfort is always to contribute to the worst.

RENÉ GIRARD
Battling to the End

Duality of Practical Reason

One of the reasons I came to take an interest in nuclear deterrence, along with many English-speaking philosophers, is that it poses the most formidable challenge to the rationalist foundations of the philosophy of action that may be imagined. Here I take as my point of departure rational choice theory and its application to strategic situations, which is to say game theory—not because I believe that game theory is competent to clear up the various dilemmas and paradoxes that figure so largely in debate on the effectiveness and the ethics of nuclear deterrence; quite to the contrary, these dilemmas and paradoxes reveal the principal inadequacy of the mode of reasoning that game theory and, more generally, rational choice theory embody without being aware of it.[1] The argument that I have developed and defended for many years now is that practical reason is twofold, not univocal. The theory of decision that underlies rational choice theory represents only one of its forms. It conceives of the time in which action takes place as a garden of forking paths, to borrow the image used by Borges in his famous story of the same name,[2] whose most common graphical representation is what is known in game theory as a decision tree. This is the most perspicuous way of representing conditional propositions of the type "If you were to do this, I would do that"—for example, threats of the type "If you were to attack me, I would answer with a nuclear strike."

Philosophically, the conception of time incarnated by a decision tree can be described as follows. While the future may be counterfactually dependent on the past, the past is always counterfactually independent of the future. Whether I decide to do this or that may have an impact on the future, but certainly not on the past: the past is fixed, whereas the future is open. There is a symmetry, in other words, between counterfactual dependencies and causal dependencies. I maintain that we have access to another type of practical reason, which rests on a very different conception of time, where an asymmetry obtains between these two types of dependency: the future is considered to be counterfactually independent of the past (even though it depends, or may depend, on it causally); the past is considered to depend counterfactually on the future (even though, necessarily, it does not depend on it causally). On this view, the future is fixed, the past is open. I have shown not only that this alternate temporality is logically coherent but that it is implicit in many theoretical constructs that nonetheless are supposed to rest on the orthodox conception. This misunderstanding of their own metaphysical basis is manifested by various paradoxes that philosophers have devoted a considerable amount of time and energy to resolving. The problem of rational expectations, in particular, can be satisfactorily dealt with only if it is seen to involve this alternate temporality. The efforts of moral philosophers such as David Gauthier to ground a deontological ethics on rational choice theory alone suffer from the same misapprehension.[3]

For the sake of convenience, I call the orthodox temporality, which assumes the future to be open and the past to be fixed, occurring time, and the alternate temporality, which assumes the future to be fixed and the past to be open, projected time. The concept of equilibrium, fundamental in the social sciences, takes on very different meanings in these two conceptions of time. In occurring time, for a game having a finite horizon, the relevant concept is so-called subgame perfect equilibrium, which is arrived at by means of backward induction, a method that came to be widely adopted in many fields with the advent of dynamic programming in the 1950s and that was thought to have a sound logical basis until a number of crippling paradoxes were discovered. In a finite-horizon game, backward induction consists in moving backward from the lowest node on the decision tree, step by step. Quite obviously it assumes occurring time: the future regards the past as fixed and is caused by it; the past, for its part, considers the mathematical function that describes the reaction of the future to the past to be fixed and acts accordingly. The past being fixed, the rationality of an action is assessed solely in relation to its consequences. As Maurice Allais put it, only the future matters.

To the subgame perfect equilibrium arrived at by backward induction there corresponds the concept of equilibrium in projected time that I call projected equilibrium.[4] Here the roles of future and past are reversed: now it is the past that considers the future to be fixed. The past anticipates the future and reacts accordingly. The future takes the function that describes the anticipation and reaction of the past to be fixed and acts accordingly.

Things are nonetheless more complicated. To be sure, the counterfactual dependencies amount to a reversal of time, but the causal dependencies continue to operate in accordance with time's arrow, the familiar direction of time. The past preserves the power to causally produce the future. A future in which a past that anticipates it causally prevents its realization would quite simply not be a conceivable future. This proposition may seem innocuous. To appreciate its importance, one needs to keep in mind that it is false in our ordinary conception of time—that is, occurring time. Why do we try to foresee the future? In order to change it, as popular wisdom has it. Taken literally, however, this claim is metaphysical nonsense. For it to be meaningful, we must say instead that what is anticipated is the future that would have been realized if it had not been anticipated, or if one had not reacted to its anticipation in the way one did. This is therefore not the actual future. It is a counterfactual conditional future, a possible future whose potentiality is not actualized. Clausewitz's famous maxim, that possible events should be judged real by reason of their consequences, is valid in occurring time: possible events have a reality even when they are not actualized, since they intervene in a process of deliberation that clarifies a choice. But this becomes false in projected time. Once history has unfolded and events have taken place, nothing is possible outside the actual.

The form assumed by projected time is therefore not that of an inverted tree. It is a circle, as we saw in the final chapter (figure 4.1). Projected equilibrium is a fixed point of the circle that connects the future to the past by means of a counterfactual link (anticipation/ reaction) and then the past to the future by means of a causal link.

What makes the debate about the effectiveness of nuclear deterrence so frustratingly inconclusive is that it mixes together arguments that do not involve the same conception of time: some are situated in occurring time, while others make sense only in projected time. Probably no problem of rational choice throws a clearer light on the duality of practical reason than nuclear deterrence.

From the Prisoner's Dilemma to the Game of Chicken

One of the great virtues of rational choice theory is that it has shown the possibility of conflicts in which, each party seeking to maximize its own interest, the result is disastrous for all—and, in particular, less beneficial than if all parties had agreed to exercise restraint and were capable of doing so. It is because they are rational that the parties prove to be incapable of resolving their differences in a way that preserves their common interests. The notion of a dominant strategy plays an important role in this paradoxical result.

In chapter 3 I mentioned two types of "game," in the technical sense that the theory of the same name gives to this word, that need to be taken into consideration in conceptualizing and formalizing situations of war: the prisoner's dilemma, which is supposed to model the war of all against all that Hobbes thought inevitable in a state of nature, and the game of chicken, which Russell saw as embodying the essence of nuclear deterrence. These two games have very different structures that it will be useful for our purposes to compare. I begin with the prisoner's dilemma.[5]

Two players, Ego and Alter, each have a choice between two strategies: to cooperate (C) or to defect (D). Four cases are therefore possible, each of which assigns a certain "payoff" to the two players; in figure A.1, Ego's payoff appears at the bottom left of each square, Alter's at the upper right. If Ego and Alter both cooperate, each receives R (Reward); if both defect, each receives P (Punishment), smaller than R. If one defects while the other cooperates, the defector receives T (Temptation), where T is greater than R, while the one who cooperates receives S (Sucker's payoff). The condition of a prisoner's dilemma, then, is T > R > P > S, where the symbol > stands for "greater than."

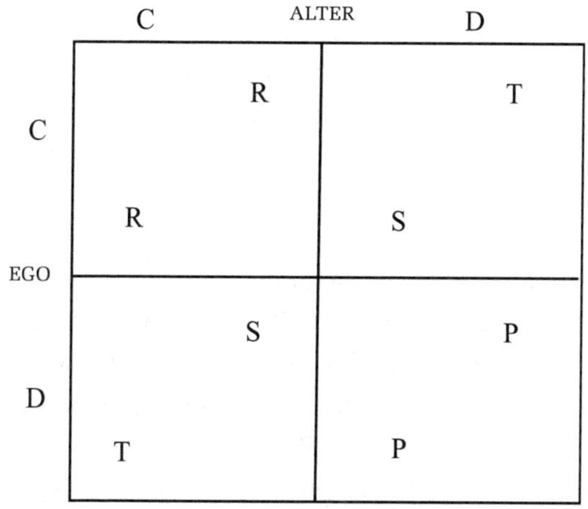

FIGURE A.1

The very great majority of theorists who have studied this structure reason as follows. I am Ego. In principle, my choice ought to depend on what Alter does, but by hypothesis, Alter acts independently of me and without my knowing what he does. I realize, however, that this is of no importance because, *whatever he does*, it is in my interest to defect: if he does C, I should do D (since T > R); if he does D, I should also do D (since P > S). In other words, I have a dominant strategy—in this case to defect.

In accordance with the principle of a dominant strategy, I find it rational to defect. Alter does as well, for he finds himself in the same situation. We both find ourselves in (D, D), which gives each of us P, whereas if we had cooperated, we would both have gotten R, a greater payoff, since R > P. The prisoner's dilemma constitutes a pragmatic paradox, since both players are condemned, for the most rational reasons imaginable, to live with the consequences of a situation that, by comparison with another possible situation, is less desirable for each of them. The mutual impasse in the square (D, D) illustrates the supposedly inevitable absurdity of a war of all against all: "And from this diffidence of one another," Hobbes says, "there is no way for any man to secure himselfe, so reasonable, as Anticipation."[6] In a situation of latent conflict, this amounts to assuming that a rival is always ready to attack you or to supplant you in the heart of your lover in the war of the sexes.[7]

The structure of the game of chicken is very different, even though the underlying mechanism is equally capable of plunging the world into the abyss. Following the same conventions as before, we have figure A.2.

Here Ego and Alter play the game we considered earlier with reference to Russell's description of it.[8] Each player can attack (A) by not deviating from the white line or renounce (r) by swerving away from it. There are two non-catastrophic states, where one attacks and the other chickens out: Ar and rA.[9] The stake is represented by 1, an arbitrary unit of measurement, but in any case the prestige one enjoys and the humiliation one avoids by not swerving is trivial by comparison with the risk that the two players take in threatening not to deviate. This is a zero-sum game—what one wins the other loses—played at the edge of the abyss, in which the abyss is represented by the negative number –N, where N is as great as you like. There is no dominant strategy here that leads the two players to embrace mutual destruction; each player seeks to be in whichever

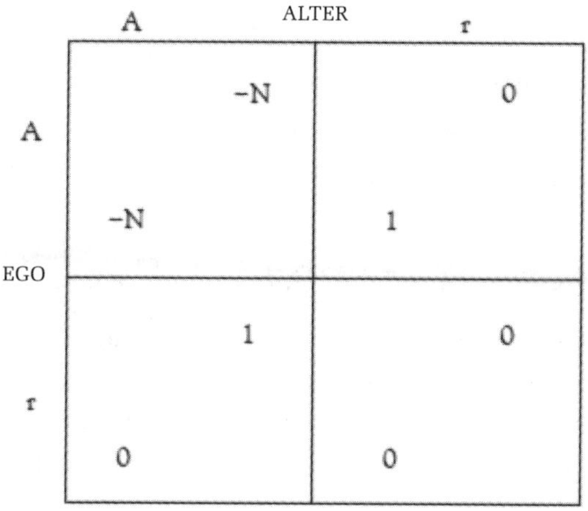

FIGURE A.2

one of the two squares Ar and rA confers prestige and avoids humiliation, at the risk of both falling into oblivion. It will be recalled that
Kennedy and Khrushchev played this immensely dangerous game
up until the very moment they reached an agreement. In spite of the
apparently childish character of such contests, they are valuable
for making us see that very often this is the way that very powerful people, and less powerful ones as well, settle their differences.
We are no longer dealing with a game in the ordinary sense of this
word, an activity involving elements of freedom and gratuitousness
that has no productive value—in a word, an unserious activity.

In the body of the text, we studied several cases where the structure of the prisoner's dilemma and that of the game of chicken led
to very different conclusions: the complex dialectic between crisis
and noncrisis stability, for example, or the nuclear arms race as a
reflection of the preponderant place occupied by the dominant strategy principle in the logic of deterrence. What nonetheless strongly
limits the interest of this type of formalization is that it lacks an essential dimension, temporality. Both games, the prisoner's dilemma
and chicken, are played in so-called normal form, which means
that the agents simultaneously choose their strategy, each one being
ignorant of the other's choice.

Let us now introduce the element of time and reformulate the logic of nuclear deterrence by considering extensive-form games, which is to say ones where the two players play in succession, one after the other. This reveals a new aspect—what Hobbes called anticipation.

Nuclear Deterrence and the MAD Structure in Game Theory

Most of the assumptions on which the debate regarding the effectiveness of nuclear deterrence is based, as well as a good number of the arguments advanced in favor of one position or another, can be elegantly and concisely represented in the decision tree in figure A.3.

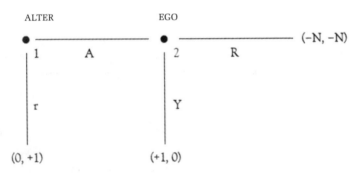

r: renounces   R: retaliates
A: attacks   Y: yields
N: very large number
Left-hand number: Alter's payoff
Right-hand number: Ego's payoff

FIGURE A.3

It can easily be seen that we are dealing here with a game of chicken in extensive form, including enormous losses ("unacceptable damage") if the players do not coordinate their behavior. The MAD structure combines this game and the one in which the positions of Alter and Ego are reversed. Attack A is a conventional (i.e.,

nonnuclear) act of aggression. Both players are vulnerable: this is
what the loss N represents for each of them. Both players are invulnerable: this is what the loss N represents *for their adversary* if the
adversary chooses the escalation R. As victims of a nuclear strike,
neither one will perish alone.

The crystal ball effect is the certainty of a double loss (−N, −N) if
one of them chooses R. The mutual assurance effect against a first
strike (or self-deterrence) is expressed as follows—where what follows, it is essential to note, assumes occurring time. Let us take as
our starting point the moment marked 2. To be sure, being at 2 implies that an attack A has taken place. But since in occurring time,
only the future matters, we are free to cut off the decision tree at any
node: the rationality of an action will be determined on the sub-tree
that branches from this point. In the present case, this sub-tree is
reduced to the bifurcation (Y, R). R would be suicidal: it is the principle of self-deterrence.

Reasoning at time 2, as we have just done, is the first stage of
backward induction. The second stage readily follows: Alter, at 1,
anticipates that if it launches a conventional attack A, Ego will not
retaliate with a nuclear strike. Alter therefore attacks. The subgame
perfect equilibrium, obtained by backward induction, is therefore
(Alter, A; Ego, Y)—or, for the parallel game not shown, (Ego, A; Alter,
Y). This equilibrium renders nuclear deterrence ineffective in the
sense that it does not assure noncrisis stability. But it renders it effective in terms of crisis stability, since nuclear conflagration is not
part of the subgame perfect equilibrium.

This is the conclusion arrived at by the critics of MAD who argue
on behalf of prudential revisionism. Furthermore, they say—what
figure A.3 cannot directly represent because it shows only one of
the two parallel games—noncrisis instability makes a conventional
war probable, which itself may lead to a nuclear conflict. Evidently
the reason for noncrisis instability in this case is the noncredible
character of the threat "If you, Alter, do A, then I, Ego, will do R"
(and vice versa). Backward induction brings out the fact that the
problem of credibility is the inevitable counterpart of the self-deterrence effect.

A good many of the arguments made in this connection therefore naturally fit into the orthodox conception of time, which forms the basis of strategic reasoning. They end up condemning nuclear deterrence from the point of view of prudence and, at the same time, of morality in each of its two branches, consequentialism and deontology. The theory of decision suited to occurring time strengthens prudential revisionism.

Two lines of argument that play a crucial role in this debate are completely neglected, however. It will become clear that they cannot even be expressed within the framework of occurring time. The first argument is due to the defenders of MAD. Let us recall Bernard Brodie's words once more, only now quoting them more fully:

> It is the curious paradox of our time that one of the foremost factors making deterrence really work and work well is the lurking fear that in some massive confrontation crisis it may fail. Under these circumstances one does not tempt fate. If we were absolutely certain that nuclear deterrence were 100 percent effective against nuclear attack, then it would cease to have much if any deterrent value against non-nuclear wars.[10]

Brodie draws our attention here to what I have called the paradox of the self-stultifying character of perfect deterrence and the attempt on the part of MAD's defenders to resolve it by introducing the element of uncertainty. I maintain that in occurring time (i.e., the time assumed by strategic thought), this argument is (a) at best, assuming it can be taken seriously, false, or (b) at worst, meaningless.

The claim is that uncertainty about the effectiveness of deterrence makes it effective. Let us suppose that this uncertainty is a strategic variable. Let us call ε the (very small) probability that Alter's (conventional) act of aggression A will lead to a nuclear conflagration and the result $(-N)$ for both adversaries. Ego might reason thus: it is rational for me to allow for an uncertainty ε such that $N\varepsilon$ is greater than 1. If Alter were to attack, its expected payoff would be 1 times $(1-\varepsilon)$ minus $N\varepsilon$, or about $1-N\varepsilon$—a negative result, as against 0 if Alter were to renounce. Assuming Alter to be rational, it therefore ought to renounce. Even so, let us assume that there is a small probability, p, that Alter, irrationally, will attack me. Allowing again for an uncertainty ε, my payoff would be 1 times (1–p) plus p times [0 times (1–ε) minus Nε], or approximately 1–p–pNε. Since Nε has an order of magnitude of 1, this result has an order of magnitude of 1–mp (where m is a positive whole number) and is therefore close to 1. If, however, Ego were to decline to exploit uncertainty as a strategic variable (which would render its deterrence ineffective, since non-credible), its payoff would be 0. Therefore it is rational for Ego to exploit uncertainty as a strategic variable.

But this reasoning is obviously false. Here uncertainty has no strategic value and does nothing to make deterrence credible. For if we were really dealing with a strategic variable, Alter could be sure that, if deterrence were to fail, Ego would not entrust the task of deciding to a lottery or a game of Russian roulette, even if they were assigned probabilities ε and 1–ε; instead Ego would yield. In a situation of mutual assured destruction, uncertainty plays no role whatever in occurring time. This is exactly what is called the crystal ball effect.

The foregoing argument is deeply confused, and moreover one that the defenders of MAD should not have been tempted to make. They rightly see that in order to make deterrence effective, it is necessary to abandon strategy—to choose not to choose. They could certainly say, in the manner made famous by Thomas Schelling and infamous by the Doomsday Machine: "Let us tie our hands, make nuclear retaliation automatic." But this would still be in the realm of strategy. The defenders of MAD are careful to say something else, if only in the form of an enigma that remains unclarified. Like Brodie, they invoke destiny, fate—not a conditional fate, expressed by a conditional proposition of the type "If you attack me, it is inevitable that I will blow up the world," for here we are still in the realm of intentions. What is more, the fated event is held to be improbable—an incomprehensible oxymoron. Apocalypse is a part of the future, but thankfully, the chance that it will occur is extremely small. These conclusions may seem sensible enough in and of themselves, but clearly they have yet to be justified in any satisfactory way.[11]

The other line of argument that cannot be expressed in occur-

ring time is pursued by the opponents of MAD, who defend prudential revisionism. The quote from Brodie can be used to introduce
this argument as well, but this time by placing emphasis on the last
sentence, which concerns the paradox of the self-stultifying character of nuclear deterrence. This paradox is a crucial element of the
case made by authors who hold that nuclear deterrence is fundamentally non-credible. Recall that the thesis of non-credibility rests
on two claims. The first insists on the absence of any presumption
effect: deterrence is not credible because it would not be rational to
carry out a nuclear threat. The second, considered the more important of the two, emphasizes the absence of any demonstration effect.
It is this second argument that appears in the form of the paradox of
self-stultification. Here it must be kept in mind that the absence of
a demonstration effect is by no means accidental; it is an essential
characteristic of nuclear deterrence. In order for deterrence to be
justified on prudential grounds, it must be absolutely effective. If its
effectiveness is absolute, there are no failures, therefore no penal-
ties for failure, and therefore no demonstration effect. As Brodie put
it, "If we were absolutely certain that nuclear deterrence were 100
percent effective against nuclear attack, then it would cease to have
much if any deterrent value against non-nuclear wars."

Let us therefore assume, for the sake of argument, that the problem created by the lack of a presumption effect can be overcome
and that deterrence is wholly effective against the risk of nuclear
conflagration. In that case, segment R, the branch of the decision
tree that leads to catastrophe, is not part of the actual world.[12] Let
us also assume, again for the sake of argument, that the reason for
this is not that Ego, playing second, does not do R, but that Alter,
playing first and doing r, does not give Ego the occasion to play. In
other words, the proposition "If you, Alter, attack me (A), then I,
Ego, will retaliate (R)" is taken seriously by Alter, who renounces.[13]
One therefore has both noncrisis and crisis stability. For the paradox of self-stultification to be preserved, it would now be necessary
to show that the assumptions we have made lead to an absurdity, in
the sense that from the non-actuality of R, due to noncrisis stability,
one ought in fact to deduce the noncrisis *instability* of deterrence,

which is to say that in fact Alter chooses to attack. Here we are in occurring time, and one could arrive at this conclusion only at the cost of a grave confusion—namely, inferring the impossibility of non-actuality. Given the assumed crisis and noncrisis stability of deterrence, R, although it is not actual, remains possible, and the fact that R is possible has effects on the actual world. This is exactly the point of Clausewitz's maxim: possible events should be judged real by reason of their consequences. To fail to see this is to fall into the sophism of those who defend deterrence by saying that although the worst has been made possible, for just this reason it will not happen; the worst is possible, but it is not actual, therefore it has no reality. It is strange to encounter this confusion in the writings and speeches of *critics* of deterrence. The younger Donald Trump did not commit this obvious logical fallacy, as the epigraph I have chosen for this book makes clear.

Supposing, then, that the absence of a presumption effect is not by itself fatal to the effectiveness of nuclear deterrence, the absence of a demonstration effect is not an argument against its effectiveness either. The paradox of self-stultification cannot be expressed in occurring time.

The two lines of argument we have just examined can nonetheless be defended, but only within the framework of projected time. Let us begin by considering the projected equilibrium of the game in question. It cannot include (Ego, R), since Alter's anticipatory reaction to that would be (Alter, r), which causally prohibits the realization of (Ego, R). By contrast, (Ego, Y), again by anticipation/reaction, gives (Alter, A), which causally links up with (Ego, Y).

The projected equilibrium is therefore (Alter, A; Ego, Y). It is identical to the subgame perfect equilibrium obtained by backward induction in occurring time. Projected equilibrium therefore also concludes that nuclear deterrence is ineffective on account of noncrisis instability, but for a fundamentally different reason: whereas the subgame perfect equilibrium deduces noncrisis instability from the absence of a presumption effect, projected equilibrium deduces it from the absence of a demonstration effect. In projected time, the sequence (Alter, r; Ego, R) is interpreted to mean that Alter renounces attacking, Ego *retaliates* with a nuclear strike—the impossibility of which is guaranteed by its absurdity. In occurring time, the interpretation of the same sequence would be that Alter renounces attacking because, if Alter were to attack, Ego would then retaliate with a nuclear strike. Ego's nuclear retaliation, although not actual since Alter renounces, would nonetheless be a possibility whose effects would make themselves felt in the actual world. In projected time, however, there is no possibility that is not actualized. Here the absurdity of Alter's renouncing and Ego's retaliating echoes the paradox of self-stultification, taking the form of a reductio ad absurdum that demonstrates the ineffectiveness of nuclear deterrence.

The objection to nuclear deterrence on prudential grounds therefore involves arguments that derive from two very different theories. As it happens, they both conclude that nuclear deterrence is ineffective. But this conclusion is contingent, as we will presently see. The deeply confused argument made by MAD's defenders in terms of an improbable fatality can be given a rigorous interpretation in projected time. On this view of the matter, uncertainty can be shown to justify nuclear deterrence on prudential grounds.

In occurring time, uncertainty can affect only a conditional counterfactual of the type "If you, Alter, were to attack me, I, Ego, would retaliate with a nuclear strike." In projected time, it is the anticipation/reaction function of the past in relation to the future that is subject to uncertainty. If Ego, acting second, were to do R, what would Alter do first? The answer to this question in occurring time is obviously that Alter, playing first, would have done A, unless Ego would not have been in a position to respond. In projected time, however, it is not the past that the future takes to be fixed, but the anticipation/reaction function of the past. Had there been no uncertainty, it would have been necessary to reply to the question thus: if Ego, playing second, were to do R, then Alter, playing first, would do r.[14] It is the causal impossibility of this response that allows us to conclude that (Ego, R) is not part of the projected equilibrium and therefore is not possible.[15]

If, however, the anticipation/reaction function of the past is affected by uncertainty, the following configuration, strange at first sight, becomes meaningful. (Ego, R) *can* be part of the projected equilibrium and thereby enjoy actual ontological status if *one* of the values taken by this function allows (Ego, R) to be causally realized. It is therefore necessary that the weight of the counterfactual conditional (If Ego were to do R, then Alter would do A) be strictly positive. This is the "probability" of the failure of deterrence in projected time. But its interpretation is radically different from that of the ε that we considered in occurring time, which signifies the probability of (If Alter, playing first, were to do A, then Ego would do R next). In occurring time, the uncertainty attaches to an intentional act: deterrence has failed, it is a fact of the past, and the question is whether Ego will now carry out its threat, bringing about a global cataclysm. In projected time, the apocalyptic fate is already part of the actual world, so to speak, for it is destined to happen. It depends on the players themselves making the likelihood of apocalypse vanishingly small by doing their utmost not to do A.

There is, then, a theory of prudence in the light of which nuclear deterrence appears to be justified. But the correlate of this prudential justification is a sentence without appeal at the court of deontological ethics.

Deontological arguments against nuclear deterrence, when they are formulated in the framework of occurring time, are never incontestable, as we have seen. There is always the possibility of an excuse or an alibi. Resort can also be had to paradoxes of the type "It is by making absolute evil possible that it can be prevented from becoming actual"—a proposition of doubtful validity, but no more doubtful than a proposition of the type "The mere fact of making absolute evil possible is an absolute evil, even if the possibility is not realized." In projected time, by contrast, things are infinitely clearer. There, absolute evil *is actual*, for it is part of the actuality of projected equilibrium. Since only the actual, and not the merely possible, is capable of acting on the actual, effective deterrence exists only if the threat is carried out in an actual future, however improbable it may be. Deontological judgment in this case is therefore in no way different from the incontestable condemnation of a nation that enters into a nuclear conflict.

Let us sum up. We are faced with two theories of prudence. The first, associated with the orthodox theory of decision, condemns nuclear deterrence not only on prudential grounds but also perhaps in respect of morality. The second, associated with projected time, succeeds in justifying nuclear deterrence on prudential grounds, but at the cost of its unambiguous condemnation on moral grounds. Theoretically, then, it is possible to regard nuclear deterrence as being both effective and rational. But this cannot hide the fact that, morally, it is an abomination.

Acknowledgments

American thinkers have made inestimable contributions to the study of nuclear war, some of the greatest philosophers of the past sixty years among them. It is to these philosophers that I am most indebted, for having tried to make sense of the unprecedented upheaval in our customary ways of thinking about the world caused by the invention of the atomic bomb—and this by drilling down to the deepest level of rational analysis: metaphysics.[1] For the present work to be translated into English is therefore a signal honor, allowing me to repay my debt to these authors, even if only in a very modest fashion. In this connection I owe special thanks to Malcolm DeBevoise, my longtime translator, whose very great talent I once more gratefully acknowledge.

Notes

Introduction

1. I have been led in particular, as we will see in chapter 4, to propose a new solution to one of the oldest metaphysical aporia, the Master Argument of Diodorus Cronus.

2. Snow should have written "mathematical necessity." A physical chemist as well as a novelist, known for his theory of the "two cultures," Snow was a powerful mind, but pardonably unfamiliar with the philosophical distinction between necessity--an ontological category--and certainty--an epistemological category.

3. Thomas C. Schelling, "An Astonishing Sixty Years: The Legacy of Hiroshima," Nobel Prize Lecture delivered at Beijersalen, The Royal Swedish Academy of Sciences, Stockholm, 8 December 2005.

4. The word *chance*, if only through its etymology, refers to the concepts of contingency and probability, which, as I go on to show, are not adequate for our purposes. For the moment, however, it will do.

5. See Scott D. Sagan, "The World's Most Dangerous Man: Putin's Unconstrained Power Over Russia's Nuclear Arsenal," *Foreign Affairs*, 16 March 2022, https://www.foreignaffairs.com/articles/russian-federation/2022-03-16/worlds-most-dangerous-man.

6. The yield of such weapons may nonetheless be as much as twenty times that of Little Boy, the bomb that destroyed Hiroshima.

7. Critics of nuclear deterrence typically assert the opposite. They hold

that nuclear deterrence is an abstract theory assuming perfect rationality on the part of actors. Since this condition cannot be satisfied in practice, they conclude that the very concept of nuclear deterrence is a nonstarter.

8. Alexei Arbatov, "Reducing the Role of Nuclear Weapons," paper presented to the International Conference on Nuclear Disarmament, Oslo, Norway, 26–27 February 2008, pp. 5-6; the emphasis is mine.

9 Reuters, Aerospace and Defense News, 28 November 2019, quoted by Brennan Deveraux, "Why Intermediate-Range Missiles Are a Focal Point in the Ukraine Crisis," *War on the Rocks*, 28 January 2002, https://warontherocks.com/2022/01/why-intermediate-range-missiles-are-a-focal-point-in-the-ukraine-crisis/.

10. I employ this rather unusual formulation deliberately, for it saves me from having to rely on the notion of probability, which, as I say, has no validity here.

11. Reuters, "Russia Must Not Be Humiliated Despite Putin's 'Historic' Mistake, Macron Says," 4 June 2022, https://www.reuters.com/world/europe/russia-must-not-be-humiliated-despite-putins-historic-mistake-macron-2022-06-04/.

Chapter 1

1. The term *ballistic*, whether or not it is associated with *missile*, will frequently recur in this book. It is therefore important that it be precisely defined. Any projectile that is subject solely to the force of terrestrial gravitation is said to be ballistic. An intercontinental missile, for example, is propelled by a rocket that allows it to attain a very high velocity. When it separates from the rocket, it is subject to gravity alone and becomes ballistic—which is to say that its path describes an ellipse one of whose foci is the center of the earth, in accordance with the laws of Newtonian mechanics. It can thus travel a distance of 10,000 kilometers (more than 6,000 miles) and, after having reached an altitude of 3,000 kilometers (almost 2,000 miles), reenter the atmosphere at a speed of 30,000 kilometers (almost 20,000 miles) per hour. In this last non-ballistic phase—the most problematic one with regard to the effectiveness of a nuclear strike because of the very substantial thermal barrier needing to be penetrated on reentry—the missile delivers the warhead. Anti-tank weapons and other short-range missiles (so-called tactical missiles), by contrast, are not ballistic because the resistance of the air through which they travel is much greater than the earth's attraction.

2. Welles's dramatized report of a Martian invasion, broadcast on the CBS radio network on 30 October 1938, panicked a good many Americans;

based on H. G. Wells's novel *The War of the Worlds*, it was presented as something real. In retrospect it is clear that Orson Welles was the inventor of fake news.

3. See Michel Foucault, *Ceci n'est pas une pipe* (Montpellier: Fata Morgana, 1973).

4. This was therefore not an instance of fake news.

5. See Cynthia Lazaroff, "Dawn of a New Armageddon," *Bulletin of the Atomic Scientists*, 6 August 2018.

6. See William J. Perry, "The Terrifying Lessons of Hawaii's Botched Missile Alert," *Politico*, 15 January 2018.

7. As against Kenneth Waltz, who defended the heterodox position that nuclear proliferation may be a good thing, Scott Sagan renewed their important debate two decades ago by rejecting an assumption that leads many people still today to doubt that nuclear war is possible. They think only of a single scenario, in which nuclear weapons are deliberately employed. Many scenarios can be imagined, however, leading to war that is the result of an accident, perhaps due to severe instability within the government of a nuclear power, for example. See Scott Sagan and Kenneth Waltz, *The Spread of Nuclear Weapons: A Debate Renewed* (New York: W. W. Norton, 2003).

8. See Carl von Clausewitz, *On War*, ed. and trans. Michael Howard and Peter Paret (Princeton, N.J.: Princeton University Press, 1976).

9. Thérèse Delpech, in *La dissuasion nucléaire au XXIe siècle* (Paris: Odile Jacob, 2012), a book that attracted wide notice in the French press, commits the classic error of drawing too sharp a distinction between deterrence and war, even though she rightly criticizes their frequent confusion. She deplores the fact that "the difference between a doctrine of deterrence and a doctrine of effective use of nuclear weapons is not recognized, with the result that nuclear deterrence is thought to be indissociable from a doctrine concerning the use of such weapons, when the purpose of deterrence is precisely to prevent them from ever being used." There is, of course, a difference between actual violence and the simulation of violence, but experience shows that simulating violence is a dangerous game that can easily degenerate into actual violence.

10. At the head of this chapter I placed an epigraph taken from William Perry's excellent book, *My Journey at the Nuclear Brink* (Stanford, Calif.: Stanford University Press, 2015). It is the conjunction in the title of the words *at* and *journey* that is interesting. *At* indicates that one is in a certain place, by contrast with *to* or *toward*, which mean that one is going somewhere. To speak of a journey at the nuclear brink therefore means something quite different than the classic image of rushing toward the abyss or simply of being right on the edge. A journey implies movement. Perry

therefore sees himself as advancing along the edge of the abyss, where the least misstep will send him to his death. The pertinence of this image will become clear in due course.

11. John Brennan, a former director of the CIA, estimated the chances of this outcome to be between 20 and 25 percent in September 2017; Richard Haas, president of the Council on Foreign Relations, ventured a higher figure, 50 percent. Probabilities of this sort do not count for much, if only because they do not specify the timing of the event in question. Was nuclear war supposed to occur before the end of Trump's first term? A more profound difficulty, as we will see, is that the concept of probability is of little or no use in this context.

12. Scott D. Sagan, "The Korean Missile Crisis: Why Deterrence Is Still the Best Option," *Foreign Affairs*, November/December 2017.

13. Notably among them—and ironically so, since he was the one who came closest to being a psychologist—is the psychoanalyst Jacques Lacan. But for the subject Lacan substituted the symbolic, which, he claimed, functions in the manner of a cybernetic machine.

14. Claude Lefort, "La question de la démocratie," in *Essais sur le politique* (Paris: Seuil, 1986); the emphasis is mine.

15. I shall return to this case in chapter 4.

16. Friedrich Nietzsche, *The Gay Science*, trans. Walter Kaufmann (New York: Vintage, 1974), §290.

17. Jean-Jacques Rousseau, *Rousseau, Judge of Jean-Jacques: Dialogues*, in *The Collected Writings of Rousseau*, ed. and trans. Roger D. Masters and Christopher Kelly, 13 vols. (Hanover, N.H.: University Press of New England, 1990–2009), 1:9; translation slightly modified.

18. See Gans's deeply insightful analysis in "Window of Opportunity," *Chronicles of Love and Resentment*, no. 248, 20 October 2001, http://www.anthropoetics.ucla.edu/views/vw248.htm.

19. Bullshit acquired the status of a philosophical concept with the appearance some years ago of a widely noticed book by the philosopher Harry G. Frankfurt, *On Bullshit* (Princeton, N.J.: Princeton University Press, 2005). Frankfurt contrasts bullshitting with lying. A liar hides the truth; a bullshitter hides the fact that he does not give a damn about the distinction between truth and falsity.

20. Dominique David, at the time the director of the Institut de stratégie militaire, quoted in the *Christian Science Monitor*, 4 June 1986.

21. The following story, whose origin is uncertain, very subtly demystifies the apparently implacable dynamic of verbal escalation. Long ago, in a small town in Poland, four tailors plied their trade in the same street. The competition between them was unrelenting. One morning, above the door of one shop, the townspeople found a sign that read: "Here is David,

the best tailor in the town." The next day his neighbor put up a sign that read: "Here is Jacob, the best tailor in the country." The day after that, the one next door to him posted this notice: "Here is Moshe, the best tailor in the world." On the morning of the fourth day, the last one of them hung a sign above his door with these words: "Here is Joshua, the best tailor in the street."

Note that if Joshua had staked his claim first, one would have taken this for an ordinary example of oneupmanship, potentially limitless. In reality, each one of the four tailors says the same thing, namely, that he is better than his three rivals. The four propositions are themselves mutually incompatible, of course; only one of the four can be the best. Thanks to Joshua, the endless and absurd ratcheting up of the scale of reference can be seen for what it is: a pure illusion that masks the harsh reality of mimetic rivalry. It is this dynamic that is responsible for converting words into weapons of mass destruction. See Hyun-Binn Cho, Tying the Adversary's Hands: Provocation, Crisis Escalation, and Inadvertent War (Ph.D. diss., University of Pennsylvania, 2018).

22. Quoted in Daniel Ellsberg, *The Doomsday Machine: Confessions of a Nuclear Planner* (New York: Bloomsbury, 2017), 271.

23. Denis Diderot magnificently analyzed this dual personality in *Paradoxe sur le comédien* (1773–1777), published posthumously in 1830.

24. It did not, however, prevent him from losing the war in Vietnam.

25. From the title of a chapter in the first volume of Günther Anders, *Die Antiquiertheit des menschen* (Munich: C. H. Beck, 1956); this text was subsequently published in French as *De la bombe et de notre aveuglement face à l'apocalypse* (Paris: Titanic, 1995).

26. Ellsberg, *The Doomsday Machine*, 3.

27. Ellsberg, *The Doomsday Machine*, 258.

28. See Gar Alperovitz, *The Decision to Use the Atomic Bomb and the Architecture of an American Myth* (New York: Knopf, 1995).

29. Barton Bernstein, "Understanding the Atomic Bomb and the Japanese Surrender: Missed Opportunities, Little-Known Near Disasters, and Modern Memory," *Diplomatic History* 19, no. 2 (1995): 227–73.

30. See Ellsberg, *The Doomsday Machine*, 269–70.

31. See Hannah Arendt, *Eichmann in Jerusalem: A Report on the Banality of Evil* (New York: Viking, 1963; rev. and aug. ed., 1965).

32. See Günther Anders, *Hiroshima ist überall: Tagebuch aus Hiroshima und Nagasaki* (Munich: C. H. Beck, 1958); published in French as *Hiroshima est partout*, trans. Ariel Morabia et al. (Paris: Seuil, 2008).

33. See Hannah Arendt, Letter to Gershom Scholem, 24 July 1961, in *The Correspondence of Hannah Arendt and Gershom Scholem*, ed. Marie-Luise Knott, trans. Anthony David (Chicago: University of Chicago Press, 2017).

See also my discussion in Jean-Pierre Dupuy, *A Short Treatise on the Meta-physics of Tsunamis*, trans. M. B. DeBevoise (East Lansing: Michigan State University Press, 2015), 43–50.

34. On the events that led to the First World War, see Christopher Clark, *The Sleepwalkers: How Europe Went to War in 1914* (London: Allen Lane, 2012).

35. Some readers may accuse me of being excessively pessimistic. After all, did not the events of 2018 show that Trump and Kim were capable of overcoming their differences, having apparently reached an agreement in principle at their meeting in Singapore on 11 June that the Korean Penin-sula should be denuclearized? I was among those who thought, before the summit took place, that Trump would come out of it looking like the greater dupe of the two and that failure to reach an agreement would considerably increase the chances of a nuclear conflict. The summit bore all the marks of a fool's bargain. Trump saw it as confirming that sanctions, in combina-tion with the violence of his threats, had achieved the desired result; Kim saw it as confirming that his country was finally recognized in the eyes of the world as a nuclear power. But now that Kim had given the impression that he wanted peace, above all with South Korea, it became difficult to threaten him with tougher sanctions, much less total annihilation. As for the notion of denuclearization, the course of events so far has shown that the two countries understand the word to mean two completely different things—not for the first time in the turbulent history of American-North Korean relations. The United States expects North Korea to renounce nuclear development completely, submitting its weapons and missiles to regular international inspection; North Korea expects the United States to dismantle the extended deterrent capability (the famous "nuclear um-brella") that had been put in place in order to guarantee the security of nonnuclear regional allies, chiefly South Korea, but also very probably Japan as well. Many experts agree that North Korea will renounce neither the maintenance nor the expansion of its nuclear forces in the foreseeable future and that if Japan were to nuclearize in response to an American pullback, it would have a domino effect, the consequences of which cannot be predicted.

Chapter 2

1. The word *strategic* will very often be met with in the pages that follow. Typically associated with missiles and nuclear weapons, it originated in the desire of the American air force to distinguish its arsenal from that of

the army, whose missiles were said to be "tactical"; see Daniel Ellsberg, *The Doomsday Machine: Confessions of a Nuclear Planner* (New York: Blooms-bury, 2017), 234. This distinction rests on technical differences in oper-ational capability, of course, but at bottom it is rooted in U.S. Air Force doctrine, which insists on the overriding need to destroy the economy, and with it the civil society, of the enemy nation.

2. Ronald Reagan, "Foreword Written for a Report on the Strategic De-fense Initiative," 28 December 1984, in *Weekly Compilation of Presidential Documents* 21, no. 1 (7 January 1985): 8–9.

3. Quoted by David Holloway in "Racing Toward Armageddon? Soviet Views of Strategic Nuclear War, 1955-1972," a paper delivered at the Nu-clear Legacies Conference held in Hiroshima, August 2017; reprinted in Michael D. Gordin and G. John Ikenberry, eds., *The Age of Hiroshima* (Princeton, N.J.: Princeton University Press, 2020).

4. The radical change in the American position that followed was in large part due to Republicans. Witness the spectacular evolution in the thinking of George Shultz, secretary of state in the Reagan Administra-tion. At that time he was among the skeptics who doubted the effective-ness of any shield whatever. On the eve of the election of George W. Bush, whom he advised informally on foreign affairs, Shultz favored a shield of reduced impenetrability, without being under any illusions with regard to its effectiveness. In the years afterward, along with William Perry, Henry Kissinger, and former Senator Sam Nunn, under the auspices of the Nu-clear Threat Initiative, he sought to bring about a world in which nuclear weapons will have completely disappeared.

5. In that same year, 2000, American experts foresaw that North Korea would be capable of threatening the American continent with ballistic mis-siles by 2005.

6. Quoted in Steven Lee Myers and Jane Perlez, "Documents Detail U.S. Plan to Alter '72 Missile Treaty," *New York Times*, 28 April 2000; the empha-sis in the last instance is mine. See also Michael R. Gordon, "In a New Era, U.S. and Russia Bicker Over an Old Issue. Missile Defense Debate: Clinton's Plan to Build Shield Against 'Rogue' States Has the Kremlin Suspicious," *New York Times*, 25 April 2000.

7. See William J. Broad, "U.S.-Russian Talks Revive Old Debates on Nu-clear Warnings," *New York Times*, 1 May 2000.

8. Thomas Hobbes, *Leviathan* 2.17. The words I have italicized, it will be noted, are anagrams.

9. The phrase was used twice by General de Gaulle, speaking at press conferences at Élysée Palace, Paris, on 14 January 1963 and 23 July 1964; quoted by Bruno Tertrais, "La dissuasion nucléaire française après la guerre froide: Continuité, ruptures, interrogations," *Annuaire français de*

relations internationales 1 (2000): 763–64.

10. These phrases appear in the *Livre blanc sur la défense nationale*, vol. 1 (Paris: Ministère de la Défense, 1972); quoted by Tertrais, "La dissuasion nucléaire française après la guerre froide," 763.

11. In military parlance, *conventional* is a synonym for "nonnuclear." There is no choice but to adopt this usage in French, which does not recognize the term in the English sense. To be sure, both languages use it literally to mean that which results from an agreement, but in English, unlike French, it also has the sense of something customary, that which is in conformity with tradition.

12. One also speaks of "mutual vulnerability," an expression that French nuclear planners seem to prefer.

13. Jonathan Schell, *The Fate of the Earth* (New York: Knopf, 1982), 307.

14. Quoted in James G. Blight, Bruce J. Allyn, and David A. Welch, *Cuba on the Brink: Castro, the Missile Crisis, and the Soviet Collapse* (New York: Rowman and Littlefield, 2002), 379; see also the account in Ellsberg, *The Doomsday Machine*, 209–10.

15. See Nina Tannenwald, *The Nuclear Taboo: The United States and the Non-Use of Nuclear Weapons since 1945* (New York: Cambridge University Press, 2009). This idea has been popularized by smugly optimistic and irresponsible media-savvy pseudo-savants such as Steven Pinker, whose best-selling book *The Better Angels of Our Nature: Why Violence Has Declined* (New York: Viking, 2011) is a concatenation of sophisms.

16. Research conducted by Scott Sagan has clearly established the nonexistence of a nuclear taboo. When the loss of human life on the American side was weighed against that on the enemy side (an argument on which the official justification for the bombing of Japan has long relied and which still today is accepted by a minority of Americans), a large majority of the persons interviewed approved of the use of atomic weapons against the civilian population of a nonnuclear power such as Iran, if by killing two million Iranian civilians, it would be possible to save the lives of twenty thousand American soldiers. See Scott D. Sagan and Benjamin A. Valentino, "Revisiting Hiroshima in Iran: What Americans Really Think about Using Nuclear Weapons and Killing Noncombatants," *International Security* 42, no. 1 (2017): 41–79.

17. It was from a neighboring island in the Marianas, Tinian, that the fleet of B-29s took off to bomb Hiroshima and Nagasaki in August 1945.

18. Quoted in Norman Cousins, "The Cuban Missile Crisis: An Anniversary," *Saturday Review*, 15 October 1977; see also Ellsberg, *The Doomsday Machine*, 220–22.

19. Valéry Giscard d'Estaing, *Le Pouvoir et la vie*, 3 vols. (Paris: France Loisirs, 1988–2006), 2:208. It happens that in this same simulated exercise,

Méry himself had decided not to fire. "Then why," Giscard wryly wondered, "was this request put to me?"

20. Giscard d'Estaing, *Le Pouvoir et la vie*, 2:210. The emphasis is mine.

21. I regret having to use the word *preempt*, an etymological barbarism (actually an anglicism), but there seems to be no alternative. In juridical language, preemption—ultimately from the Latin *emptio*, meaning "purchase"—signifies the right of purchasing before others. In English, and by contamination in French, "preemption" has come to signify the fact of seizing the initiative, no matter what the context, the reference to purchasing having been wholly forgotten. In French, an etymologically more respectable translation is *prévention*, but this misses an important distinction for strategic thought. Preemption in the English sense of the term implies that an enemy attack is imminent, indeed that it may already have begun, and that, on being alerted by a warning system, one side launches its own missiles in reaction to an event whose future existence is considered so probable that it is taken to be an actual fact, while at the same time seeking to prevent it from happening—an enormous paradox, which I shall try to elucidate in chapter 4. Prevention, by contrast, supposes that the threat one seeks to avert is a possibility in the future, a probable or even a very probable one, and that one makes the first move by taking what is called preventive action. In this case there is no paradox. In military usage in English, *preventive* is usually associated with war whereas *preemptive* is associated with an attack.

22. Ellsberg, *The Doomsday Machine*, 20; emphasis in the original.

23. Ellsberg, *The Doomsday Machine*, 12; emphasis in the original.

24. Ellsberg, *The Doomsday Machine*, 13.

25. More than anything else, an extraordinary omission brings out the singular character of Ellsberg's astonishing book. The index contains no entry for either deterrence or mutual assured destruction. Naturally the word *deterrence* appears here and there in the text, but nowhere is it treated as a key concept. This is absolutely unprecedented in the very rich literature on atomic weapons.

26. See Ellsberg, *The Doomsday Machine*, 322.

27. This structure will be examined in greater detail in the following chapters; see also the appendix.

28. See Douglas R. Hofstadter, *Gödel, Escher, Bach: An Eternal Golden Braid* (New York: Basic Books, 1979).

29. See Ellsberg, *The Doomsday Machine*, 213–17. For a somewhat different version of these events see Svetlana V. Savranskaya, "New Sources on the Role of Soviet Submarines in the Cuban Missile Crisis," *Journal of Strategic Studies* 28, no. 2 (2005): 233–59. I am grateful to an anonymous reviewer for drawing my attention to this article. Nevertheless I have pre-

ferred Ellsberg's more recent account on the whole.

30. The linguistic and metaphysical tool that permits a comparison to be made between the actual world and another possible world is called a counterfactual proposition. A conditional proposition of the type "if x, then y" may be indicative ("If it rains tomorrow, I will not go to work") or counterfactual ("If I were rich, I would buy myself a Lamborghini"). The term *counterfactual* refers to the presence of an antecedent ("if I were rich") that is contrary to fact (alas, I am not richer than I am). The truth values of these two types of conditionals are quite different. To take a classic example, the proposition "If Shakespeare did not write *Hamlet*, someone else did" is indubitably true since the play exists and necessarily it has an author. By contrast, to assert the truth of the counterfactual proposition "If Shakespeare had not written *Hamlet*, someone else would have" is highly problematic; many may feel that only the Bard's genius could have produced this masterpiece.

31. Herman Kahn, *On Thermonuclear War* (Princeton, N.J.: Princeton University Press, 1960).

32. See Ellsberg, *The Doomsday Machine*, 64–65.

33. A fractal structure or form is similar to itself at any scale. A potentially infinite branching may exhibit self-similarity, for example.

34. Bruno Tertrais, interviewed by Étienne Jacob, "Qu'est-ce que le 'bouton nucléaire' brandi par Donald Trump et Kim Jong-un?," *Le Figaro*, 3 February 2018.

35. In their book *L'Illusion nucléaire: La face cachée de la bombe atomique* (Paris: Éditions Charles Léopold Mayer, 2018), Paul Quilès (minister of defense under François Mitterrand), Jean-Marie Collin, and Michel Drain mention an almost farcical debate on the subject of French-style delegation. They quote an anonymous journalist as saying that "in case of war, special procedures are provided for so that the order to use nuclear weapons can be delegated in emergency situations," and that, in General de Gaulle's time, delegation could be made to "someone, perhaps in the provinces, whose identity was kept secret." This, the journalist suggested, could still be the case today. You'd think you were dreaming. The authors conclude (p. 67): "An official clarification would nonetheless be welcome!" What no one grasps here is the point made by Ellsberg: a secret of this sort is a strategic absurdity.

36. See Jean-Pierre Dupuy, *Retour de Tchernobyl: Journal d'un homme en colère* (Paris: Seuil, 2006).

37. Thus the title of chapter 19 of his book; see Ellsberg, *The Doomsday Machine*, 297–308.

38. See Ellsberg, *The Doomsday Machine*, 305–6.

39. Ellsberg, *The Doomsday Machine*, 307.

40. The Strategic Arms Reduction Treaty (START), signed by George H. W. Bush and Mikhail Gorbachev.

41. "Will someone from his depleted and food starved regime," Trump tweeted on 2 January 2018, "please inform him that I too have a Nuclear Button, but it is a much bigger & more powerful one than his, and my Button works!"

42. The famous "missile gap." On this improbable error, see Ellsberg's passionate recollection, *The Doomsday Machine*, 158–68. Here again Ellsberg was not only a theorist but an actor.

43. See the belated French translation of Anders's 1958 book, *La Menace nucléaire: Considérations radicales sur l'âge atomique*, trans. Christophe David (Paris: Le Serpent à plumes, 2006), especially chapter 2.

44. The welcome and timely book demystifying atomic weapons by Quilès, Collin, and Drain, *L'Illusion nucléaire*, includes among the "false certainties" on which this illusion was built the idea that France's claim to a seat on the Security Council depended on having nuclear weapons. The authors remind us that the charter of the United Nations, which created the council, was adopted on 26 June 1945 and that the council was convened for the first time on 17 January 1946. Of its five permanent members (China, France, the Soviet Union, the United Kingdom, and the United States), only the last one possessed nuclear weapons; France did not acquire a nuclear capability until 1960. Quite true. Nevertheless, it is curious that a book that sets out to expose the nuclear illusion and discredit "the idea that nuclear weapons are a mark of prestige" does not see that there is, if not a relation of historical causality, at least a correlation between the fact of possessing the bomb and the illusion of power to which this gives rise. After all, the word *prestige* says exactly that. It comes from the Latin *praestigium*, meaning "illusion"—whence our word *prestidigitator*. True demystification in this case consists in saying, as Anders does, that nuclear weapons are indeed a mark of prestige, but the prestige amounts to nothing.

45. A professor of history at Stanford and, like Martin Hellman, a member of the Center for International Security and Cooperation (CISAC) there, Holloway is an internationally recognized authority on Soviet (later Russian) nuclear history. In his paper delivered at Hiroshima in 2017 (see n. 3), he could not help but dwell on American nuclear history, so closely did each of these violent twins monitor the movements of the other.

46. These lines actually occur in a 1945 essay that appeared in expanded form the following year in Bernard Brodie, ed., *The Absolute Threat* (New York: Harcourt, Brace, 1946), 76.–Trans.

47. Bernard Brodie, *Strategy in the Nuclear Age* (Princeton, N.J.: Princeton University Press, 1959), 408–9.

Chapter 3

1. In this chapter, the text is explicitly organized in sections and subsections having a branching structure.

2. I rely extensively in what follows on the indispensable work of Steven P. Lee, *Morality, Prudence, and Nuclear Weapons* (New York: Cambridge University Press, 1993), a unique synthesis of thinking about nuclear strategy, as much with regard to ethics as to rationality. I shall nonetheless be led, in the final chapter of this book, to disagree with his conclusions.

3. Game theory, in particular, gained fresh impetus with the publication of Thomas Schelling's seminal work, *The Strategy of Conflict* (Cambridge, Mass.: Harvard University Press, 1960).

4. Lee, *Morality, Prudence, and Nuclear Weapons*, 9.

5. Robert Jervis, *The Illogic of American Nuclear Strategy* (Ithaca, N.Y.: Cornell University Press, 1984), 26. The emphasis is mine.

6. See Jean-Pierre Dupuy, "Rational Choice Theory," in Robert A. Wilson and Frank C. Keil, eds., *MIT Encyclopedia of the Cognitive Sciences* (Cambridge, Mass.: MIT Press, 1999), 694–96.

7. See Gregory S. Kavka, *Moral Paradoxes of Nuclear Deterrence* (New York: Cambridge University Press, 1987).

8. One option is said to dominate another if it produces consequences having at least equal value for each criterion of judgment and a greater value for at least one criterion. If one option dominates all others in this sense, it is said to be the dominant option (or strategy).

9. See Kavka, *Moral Paradoxes of Nuclear Deterrence*, 20; also Russell Hardin, "Deterrence and Moral Theory," in Kenneth Kipnis and Diana T. Meyers, eds., *Political Realism and International Morality: Ethics in the Nuclear Age* (Boulder, Colo.: Westview, 1987), 35–60.

10. Jefferson McMahan, "Deterrence and Deontology," in Russell Hardin, John J. Mearsheimer, Gerald Dworkin, and Robert E. Goodwin, eds., *Nuclear Deterrence: Ethics and Strategy* (Chicago: University of Chicago Press, 1985), 158.

11. See Jean-Pierre Dupuy, *Le sacrifice et l'envie: Le libéralisme aux prises avec la justice sociale* (Paris: Calmann-Lévy, 1992).

12. See David Kreps and Robert Wilson, "Reputation and Imperfect Information," *Journal of Economic Theory* 27, no. 2 (1982): 253–79.

13. The importance of the concept of common knowledge in rational choice theory, game theory, and several key branches of cognitive science has long been well established. See Jean-Pierre Dupuy, "Common Knowledge, Common Sense," *Theory and Decision* 27, no. 1 (1989): 37–62.

14. See "From the Prisoner's Dilemma to the Game of Chicken" in the appendix. In the prisoner's dilemma, each player has a dominant strategy

in the sense defined in n. 8 above, which is to attack. Whether or not the other is prepared to attack, it is in each one's interest to take the initiative. Since both players find themselves in the same situation, the result is war.

15. The name comes from the game played in Nicholas Ray's 1955 film *Rebel Without a Cause*, starring James Dean. In a book published four years later, one of the hottest moments of the Cold War, the great philosopher and mathematician Bertrand Russell refers to this game. In the appendix, we will see how it can be formalized in game-theoretic terms; in the meantime it is worth quoting at length from Russell's account (*Common Sense and Nuclear Warfare* [New York: Simon & Schuster, 1959], 30), so perfectly does it sum up the madness of MAD:

> Since the nuclear stalemate became apparent, the Governments of the East and the West have adopted the policy which Mr. Dulles calls "brinkmanship." This is a policy adapted from a sport which, I am told, is practised by some youthful degenerates. This sport is called "Chicken!" It is played by choosing a long straight road with a white line down the middle and starting two very fast cars towards each other from opposite ends. Each car is expected to keep the wheels of one side on the white line. As they approach each other, mutual destruction becomes more and more imminent. If one of them swerves from the white line before the other, the other, as he passes, shouts "Chicken!", and the one who has swerved becomes an object of contempt. As played by irresponsible boys, this game is considered decadent and immoral, though only the lives of the players are risked. But when the game is played by eminent statesmen, who risk not only their own lives but those of many hundreds of millions of human beings, it is thought on both sides that the statesmen on one side are displaying a high degree of wisdom and courage, and only the statesmen on the other side are reprehensible. This, of course, is absurd. Both are to blame for playing such an incredibly dangerous game. The game may be played without misfortune a few times, but sooner or later it will come to be felt that loss of face is more dreadful than nuclear annihilation. The moment will come when neither side can face the derisive cry of "Chicken!" from the other side. When that moment is come, the statesmen of both sides will plunge the world into destruction.

16. Lee, *Morality, Prudence, and Nuclear Weapons*, 126.

17. See David Gauthier, "Deterrence, Maximization, and Rationality," *Ethics* 94, no. 3 (1984): 474–95; reprinted in Hardin et al., eds., *Nuclear Deterrence*, 99–120.

18. See Lee, *Morality, Prudence, and Nuclear Weapons*, 133.

19. See Gregory S. Kavka, "The Toxin Puzzle," *Analysis* 43, no. 1 (1983): 33–36. The conversation reported in the next paragraph, setting out the terms of the deal Kavka describes, is my own paraphrase.

20. Again, in the precise sense given in n. 8 above.

21. See Gregory S. Kavka, "Some Paradoxes of Deterrence," *Journal of Philosophy* 75, no. 6 (1978): 285–302.

22. Bernard Brodie, *Strategy in the Missile Age* (Princeton, N.J.: Princeton University Press, 1959), 272.

23. Leon Wieseltier, *Nuclear War, Nuclear Peace* (New York: Holt, Rinehart & Winston, 1983), quoted in Lee, *Morality, Prudence, and Nuclear Weapons*, 136.

24. Recall that *vulnerable* in this context means vulnerable to the risk that one's society will be destroyed.

25. Walter Stein, "The Limits of Nuclear War: Is a Just Deterrence Strategy Possible?," in *Peace, the Churches, and the Bomb*, ed. James Finn (New York: Council on Religion and International Affairs, 1965), 80–81; emphasis in the original omitted.

26. See Robert Jervis, *The Meaning of the Nuclear Revolution: Statecraft and the Prospect of Armageddon* (Ithaca, N.Y.: Cornell University Press, 1989), 13–14.

27. See n. 13 above.

28. "The Hydrogen Bomb: Churchill's last major speech in Parliament" (1 March 1955), *Hansard*, 5th series, vol. 537, cc. 1893.

29. Quoted by Lee, *Morality, Prudence, and Nuclear Weapons*, 239, 388n32.

30. Dominant in the technical sense, once more, that this is the best strategy regardless of what the adversary's strategy may be.

31. See Jervis, *The Meaning of the Nuclear Revolution*, 74–106.

32. These advances are associated with the concept of sequential equilibrium developed by David Kreps, Paul Milgrom, John Roberts, and Robert Wilson; see for example Kreps and Wilson, "Reputation and Imperfect Information."

33. See Jervis, *The Illogic of American Nuclear Strategy*, 148–50.

34. See Daniel Ellsberg, *The Doomsday Machine: Confessions of a Nuclear Planner* (New York: Bloomsbury, 2017), 297–308.

35. David K. Lewis, "Finite Counterforce," in *Nuclear Deterrence and Moral Restraint: Critical Choices for American Strategy*, ed. Henry Shue (New York: Cambridge University Press, 1989), 67–68.

36. Lee, *Morality, Prudence, and Nuclear Weapons*, 248.

37. Lewis, "Finite Counterforce," 74–75.

38. See George H. Quester, "The Necessary Moral Hypocrisy of the Slide into Mutual Assured Destruction, in Shue, *Nuclear Deterrence and Moral Restraint*, 227–69.

39. Jervis, *The Meaning of the Nuclear Revolution*, 98.

40. See Jean-Pierre Dupuy, *The Mark of the Sacred*, trans. M. B. DeBevoise (Stanford, Calif.: Stanford University Press, 2013), 185.

Chapter 4

1. See Jean-Pierre Dupuy, "MAD-Made World," *Inference: International Review of Science* 3, no. 3 (2017), and subsequent commentary https://inference-review.com/article/mad-made-world.

2. The principles of justice established by John Rawls in *A Theory of Justice* (Cambridge, Mass.: Harvard University Press, 1971)—a purely secular and rationalist theory that is supposed to express in an explicit and systematic fashion the conceptions of justice to which citizens of democratic nations must subscribe, so long as they understand them in the manner indicated by the author—prohibit sacrificing either the well-being or the lives of some in the name of a higher interest.

3. Gregory S. Kavka, *Moral Paradoxes of Nuclear Deterrence* (New York: Cambridge University Press, 1987), 48.

4. David K. Lewis, "Finite Counterforce," in *Nuclear Deterrence and Moral Restraint: Critical Choices for American Strategy*, ed. Henry Shue (New York: Cambridge University Press, 1989), 68.

5. See René Girard, *Violence and the Sacred* [1972], trans. Patrick Gregory (Baltimore: Johns Hopkins University Press, 1977).

6. See for example Robert McNamara and J. G. Blight, *Wilson's Ghost: Reducing the Risk of Conflict, Killing, and Catastrophe in the 21st Century* (New York: Public Affairs, 2001); also the splendid documentary made in collaboration with the filmmaker Errol Morris under the Clausewitzian title *The Fog of War: Eleven Lessons from the Life of Robert S. McNamara* (2003).

7. See Carl Schmitt, *The Nomos of the Earth in the International Law of the Jus Publicum Europaeum* [1950], trans. G. L. Ulmen (Candor, N.Y.: Telos Press, 2003).

8. "Since each man looks upon his fellow men only as though they were animals of another species, he can carry off the prey of the weaker man or give his own up to the strongest man, without considering these depradations as anything other than natural events, without the least feeling of insolence or chagrin, and without any passion other than sorrow or joy at a good or bad outcome." Jean-Jacques Rousseau, *Discourse on the Origin and the Foundations of Inequality Among Men* [1755], n. 15 (= *Œuvres Complètes*, 5 vols. [Paris: Gallimard, 1959–1995], 3:219–20).

9. In German the word usually signifies "serenity" or "calm," but I use it here in the sense that Heidegger gives it, as a relaxation of the will—that is, the necessary condition for what he called meditative thinking to flourish. I distort this sense by considering its dark side.

10. Günther Anders, in *Hiroshima est partout* [1958], trans. Ariel Morabia et al. (Paris: Seuil, 2008), 171–72.

11. The exchange occurred as part of a Town Hall moderated by Chris Matthews and broadcast by MSNBC on 30 March 2016.

12. Jacques Chirac, for example, after the resumption of French nuclear tests in the Pacific during the summer of 1995.

13. See Jonathan Schell, *The Abolition* (New York: Knopf, 1985), 151–53; also my discussion in the final section of this chapter, "Violence in Conflict with Itself."

14. Bernard Brodie, *War and Politics* (New York: Macmillan, 1973), 430–31. The emphasis is mine.

15. In what follows I will use the more compact formulation *necessary future*.

16. See Gregory Bateson, "A Theory of Play and Fantasy," in *Steps to an Ecology of Mind: Collected Essays in Anthropology, Psychiatry, Evolution, and Epistemology* (Chicago: University of Chicago Press, 1972), part 4, section 2: "The playful nip denotes the bite, but it does not denote what would be denoted by the bite."

17. See Pierre Clastres, *Archéologie de la violence: La guerre dans les sociétés primitives* (La Tour d'Aigues, France: Éditions de l'Aube, 1977).

18. See René Girard, *The Scapegoat* [1982], trans. Yvonne Freccero (Baltimore: Johns Hopkins University Press, 1986).

19. Having more than once myself quoted the following passage, I apologize in advance to readers who are already familiar with it. My only justification for doing so again is its extraordinary eloquence.

20. Quoted in Thierry Simonelli's subtle introduction to the man and his work, *Günther Anders: De la désuétude de l'homme* (Paris: Éditions Jasmine, 2004), 84–85; the emphasis is mine. Anders's German text constitutes the first chapter of *Endzeit und Zeitenende* (Munich: Beck, 1972). Anders told the story of the flood elsewhere and in other forms, particularly in *Hiroshima ist überall* (Munich: Beck, 1982).

21. Jean de la Bruyère, *Les Caractères* [1687], 11.38 (Paris: H. Didier, 1933).

22. Yascha Mounk, "The Past Week Proves That Trump Is Destroying Our Democracy," *New York Times*, 1 August 2017.

23. Another example may be found in Henry de Montherlant's play *La guerre civile* (1965). Montherlant imagines this conversation between Pompey and Cato, his general, about Caesar:

Cato: When Caesar crossed the Rubicon, there was not a town that did not welcome him with open arms. His supporters increase in number each day. They say: "Resistance is futile. Caesar is inevitable."

Pompey: These are the words of cowards. Once someone stands in his way, Caesar will no longer be inevitable.

Cato: But no one stands in his way.

Fate, in other words, is the sum of our individual failures to act.

24. See David K. Lewis, *On the Plurality of Worlds* (Oxford: Blackwell, 1986); and Robert Stalnaker, *Ifs: Conditionals, Belief, Decision, Chance, and Time* (Dordrecht: D. Reidel, 1981). In modal logic, given an adequate definition of a possible world, a state of affairs is possible if it is true in at least one possible world; necessary if it is true in all possible worlds; impossible if it is false in all possible worlds; and contingent if it is possible but not necessary. In what follows I am chiefly interested in the theory developed by Lewis, which has the virtue from the point of view of my own analysis of granting a concrete reality to possible worlds, rather than treating them as mere abstractions.

25. David K. Lewis, "Are We Free to Break the Laws?," *Theoria* 47 (1981): 113.

26. A rule of inference in the classical propositional calculus: if p implies q and p is true, then q is true.

27. The symbolic language of formal logic, whether applied to metaphysics or not, has no other utility than to express an argument in condensed form. For readers who find it incomprehensible, here is an ordinary language transcription:

N1: There is nothing that S can do at t_2 such that, if he were to do it, C would not have been the case at t_1.

N2: There is nothing that S can do at t_2 such that, if he were to do it, the link between C being the case at t_1 and his doing x at t_2 would be invalidated.

N3: There is nothing that S can do at t_2 such that, if he were to do it, he would not do x at t_2. In other words, S does indeed do x at t_2, but he is not free to act otherwise.

28. Lewis, "Are We Free to Break the Laws?," 115.
29. Lewis, "Are We Free to Break the Laws?," 113.
30. Lewis, "Are We Free to Break the Laws?," 114.
31. Alvin Plantinga, "On Ockham's Way Out," *Faith and Philosophy* 3 (1986): 243.
32. My teacher Maurice Allais, one of the founders of neoclassical economics and long the only French economist to have been awarded the Nobel Prize, used to say, "When it comes to rationality, the fundamental maxim is: *only the future matters.*" Obviously he did not mean that the past is not important. What he meant was that the past will always be what it was, and that any present action is incapable of changing this.
33. This paradox bears some resemblance to the so-called grandfather paradox, which depends on assuming the possibility of time travel: if I could travel to the past and kill my grandfather, then I would not exist.

Unlike what is implied by assuming a counterfactual power over the past, however, this way of reasoning needlessly appeals to causal relations.

34. This line occurs in the screenplay of *Minority Report*, the 2002 film by Steven Spielberg based on Philip K. Dick's story "The Minority Report," *Fantastic Universe* (1 January 1956); reprinted in *The Minority Report and Other Classic Stories* (New York: Citadel, 1996), 71–102. Dick's story, which anticipated what is now called predictive policing, illustrates in an elegant and profound fashion some of the ideas we are considering. In an undated future, operating on the basis of invariably accurate predictions made by a trio of mutants known as "precogs," the police arrest criminals just before they commit their crime—causing them to proclaim their innocence ("But I haven't done anything!"). Note that there is a paradox here only because it is postulated that the predicted future (in this case, a crime) not only will occur, but could not not occur; in philosophical terms, the future is fixed, in the sense that it is counterfactually independent of the actions that precede it. This is not true of traffic forecasts displayed electronically on road signs, for example, which do not say what the future will be, only *what it would be* if drivers were to ignore the predictions that are publicly communicated in this manner.

35. The term refers to a certain relationship to the future that was conceived by the French philosophers Gaston Berger and Bertrand de Jouvenel in the late 1950s. Known elsewhere as the "scenario method," or, more vaguely, "futurology," it is based on the idea that "all who claim to foretell or forecast the future are inevitably liars, for the future is not written anywhere—it is still to be built." Michel Godet and Fabrice Roubelat, "Creating the Future: The Use and Misuse of Scenarios," *Long Range Planning* 29, no. 2 (1996): 164.

36. I recommend the English version of this work, which is more complete and corrects a few errors. See Jules Vuillemin, *Necessity or Contingency: The Master Argument* (Stanford, Calif.: CSLI Publications, 1996).

37. Recall Aristotle's argument regarding a sea battle in chapter 9 of *On Interpretation* (19a30): "[I]t is necessary for there to be or not be a sea battle tomorrow; but it is not necessary for a sea battle to take place tomorrow, nor for one not to take place." *The Complete Works of Aristotle*, ed. Jonathan Barnes, 2 vols. (Princeton, N.J.: Princeton University Press, 1984).

38. Henri Poincaré, *Science and Hypothesis* [1902], trans. William John Greenstreet (New York: Dover, 1952), 50; see also Poincaré, "On the Foundations of Geometry," *The Monist* 9, no. 1 (1898): 42.

39. Hence the paradoxes of backward induction. See Jean-Pierre Dupuy, "Philosophical Foundations of a New Concept of Equilibrium in the Social Sciences: Projected Equilibrium," *Philosophical Studies* 100 (2000): 323–45.

40. See Jean-Pierre Dupuy [2002], *How to Think about Catastrophe:*

Toward a Theory of Enlightened Doomsaying, trans. Malcolm DeBevoise and Mark Anspach (East Lansing: Michigan State University Press, 2022).

41. This problem does not always have a solution, as Jonah, the Biblical prophet of the eighth century BCE, was well aware. Jonah had refused to prophesy the fall of Nineveh, for he knew that if he did so, in obedience to Yahweh's command, the people of Nineveh would repent and Yahweh would forgive them. Jonah chose instead to flee and hide himself from the sight of his God.

42. The fact that he shares a name with the Biblical prophet is one of those historical coincidences that seem as though they could not possibly be the result of chance. Both these prophets of doom ran up against the same theoretical obstacle, but responded to it in quite different ways. See Dupuy, *How to Think about Catastrophe*, 105–14.

43. Hans Jonas, *The Imperative of Responsibility: In Search of an Ethics for the Technological Age* (Chicago: University of Chicago Press, 1985), 113–14.

44. A poll, by making the state of public opinion known to the public, alters this very state. When a new poll is taken, some respondents, taking note of the prior results, may be inclined to prefer the winner of the earlier poll; others, as Montesquieu long ago suggested, may try to redress the balance by throwing their support behind the runner-up. It is in order to avoid such effects that polling is prohibited in some countries in the days just before an election. In a famous article published in 1954, Herbert Simon, a future Nobel laureate in economics and a pioneer of artificial intelligence, showed that the dynamics of public opinion produces a fixed point—that is, a state of opinion that remains stable when it is informed of its own state. The problem is that Simon did more than this: he showed that there are, in general, not one but several fixed points. If a polling organization wishes to give the impression that it is able to predict the future without thereby affecting the actual course of events, it must compute and announce one of the fixed points so that public knowledge of the predicted state will not change it. There is a risk, however, that public opinion will nonetheless be manipulated, since in choosing one fixed point rather than another, the pollsters interfere with the experience of projected time. See Herbert A. Simon, "Bandwagon and Underdog Effects and the Possibility of Election Predictions," *Public Opinion Quarterly* 18, no. 3 (1954): 245–53.

45. This is the reasoning adopted by all strategists, policymakers, and economists in analyzing any sequential problem having an end point. One starts from this point and works backward in time in order to infer an optimal course of action.

46. In reality the situation is much more complicated, as we have seen.

47. Recall that this is the negation of the third axiom of Diodorus Cronus.

48. In French, the verb meaning "to fail," *échouer*, initially had the nautical sense of running aground—sinking as the result of an accident. By extension, probably under the influence of the etymologically unrelated word *échec*, it came to mean "not to succeed, to prove unsuccessful." The English verb *to fail* comes from the French *faillir*, whose initial meaning was "to make a mistake, to commit an error"—or, as we would say today in a nuclear context, "to miscalculate." Later *faillir* came to mean "almost" in expressions such as *j'ai failli tomber* (I almost fell). Something bad happened, or came very close to happening, because of an error; in the same context, in English, one speaks of a "near miss" or a "near hit." In what follows I subsume all these meanings under the word *accident*, taken in its philosophical and etymological sense: that which occurs without being the result of an agent's will. The natural metaphysical habitat of accident is occurring time. Here I examine what happens when *accidental* events are relocated to projected time.

49. Savage influentially argued that a decision under uncertainty is rational if and only if it maximizes expected utility, where this magnitude is obtained by multiplying expected gains and losses by so-called subjective probabilities; the probabilities are subjective in the sense that they do not represent the objective uncertainty of phenomena but the rationality of agents in the face of an uncertain future. This rationality itself implies that agents, no matter what their preferences may be, behave in conformity with a certain number of axioms whose validity is universally accepted. Since the publication of Savage's major work, *The Foundations of Statistics* (New York: John Wiley & Sons, 1954), the theory of expected utility has been strongly criticized while yet remaining the tool most commonly used by decisionmakers and strategists everywhere.

50. See my discussion of vanishing magnitudes in the section immediately following. By convention, epsilon designates an infinitely small magnitude.

51. Strictly speaking, epsilon cannot be construed as a probability in the traditional sense, which presupposes a partition of the set of all possible cases into disjoint subsets: a given case either belongs or does not belong to a given subset. This is not the case in projected time, due to the principle of superposition. For want of a deeper analysis of this very complex concept, I use the vague notion of "weight."

52. See Dupuy, "Philosophical Foundations of a New Concept of Equilibrium in the Social Sciences."

53. This is the thesis that I defended in my 2002 book, only just now published in English as *How To Think about Catastrophe: Toward a Theory of Enlightened Doomsaying* (see n. 40 supra), in connection with the prospect of calamities that cast a dark shadow over the future of humanity as a consequence of climate change, environmental degradation, loss of biodiver-

sity, and technological and industrial accidents, in addition to the threat of nuclear war itself. The expression "enlightened doomsaying" (*catastrophisme éclairé*) has come to enjoy a certain vogue in France, where the book met with considerable commercial success; all the more likely, then, was it that the ideas I advanced would be misinterpreted and caricatured by critics, who found it a simple matter to confuse those who had read only the book's title. I was supposed to be arguing that catastrophe is *certain*, and this in order to persuade people to join together in combatting it. But if that were my purpose, the book's thesis would be absurd. For if catastrophe is certain, there is nothing to be done except to give up. In a sense, this is exactly the opposite of what I was arguing. The occurrence of catastrophe, far from being certain, must be regarded instead as indeterminate—indeterminacy being the most radical form of uncertainty. By conceiving of this absolute uncertainty as a superposition of states, it becomes possible, exclusively in the case of major catastrophes, to justify the type of prudence whose contours I sketched two decades ago in this book and later filled out in a number of other writings. Since catastrophe is both part of the future and not part of the future, it is part of the future—A *and* B, in good logic, implying A. It is inevitable, but it may not happen, as Borges put it. God, he added, keeps watch in the intervals. Replace "God" with "mankind" and we have the program of enlightened doomsaying (an expression that I myself never use any more, even if, as here, I sometimes find it necessary to mention it). In the following sections and the appendix, I try to express these ideas more rigorously and, I hope, more clearly.

54. *Dual*, in the mathematical and logical sense of the term, refers to pairwise and reciprocal properties: N being a very great number and epsilon a very small magnitude, the first question can be symbolized by the expression εN and the second by $N\varepsilon$.

55. Derek Parfit, *Reasons and Persons* (Oxford: Clarendon Press, 1984), 75.

56. See Jean-Pierre Dupuy, *Retour de Tchernobyl: Journal d'un homme en colère* (Paris: Seuil, 2006).

57. The mission of the International Atomic Energy Agency (IAEA), awarded the Nobel Peace Prize in 2005, is "to accelerate and enlarge the contribution of atomic energy to peace, health, and prosperity throughout the world." See https://www.iaea.org/about/overview/history.

58. United Nations Department of Public Information, "Chernobyl: The True Scale of the Accident," 5 September 2005, https://www.un.org/press/en/2005/dev2539.doc.htm.

59. United Nations Office for the Coordination of Humanitarian Affairs (OCHA), "Chernobyl: A Continuing Catastrophe" (April 2000), https://www.sortirdunucleaire.org/IMG/pdf/ocha-2000-chernobyl_a_continuing_catastrophe.pdf.

60. The name given to the 600,000 to 800,000 civilian and military personnel who extinguished the fire and then erased ("liquidated") all traces of the accident.

61. See Georges Charpak, Richard L. Garwin, and Venance Journé, *De Tchernobyl en Tchernobyls* (Paris: Odile Jacob, 2005). The effect of small amounts of radioactivity on human health is unknown; the considerable sums spent on research in this connection are the manifest sign of our ignorance.

62. Also known as the sorites paradox, from the Greek word *sōros*, meaning "heap." The paradox is usually expressed in terms of grains of sand, but it may be stated in many different ways.

63. The English verb *to vanish*, meaning "to disappear, dissipate, fade away," has the same etymology as the French word I use to translate "vanishingly small," *évanescent*, both deriving from the Latin verb *vanescere*, itself derived from *vanus*, meaning "empty."

64. The metaphysical principle of the identity of indiscernibles stipulates that if two entities have the same properties, then they are one and the same.

65. Quoted in Ellen Goodman, "Numbers Won't Decide the Election," *Boston Globe*, 30 November 2000.

66. See Daniel Ellsberg, *The Doomsday Machine: Confessions of a Nuclear Planner* (New York: Bloomsbury, 2017), 277–78.

67. Ellsberg, *The Doomsday Machine*, 279.

68. See Ellsberg, 280–82.

69. Quoted in Ellsberg, 276–77; the emphasis is Ellsberg's.

70. See Maurice Allais, "Le comportement de l'homme rationnel devant le risque: Critique des postulats et axiomes de l'École américaine," *Econometrica* 21, no. 4 (1953): 503–46; and Daniel Ellsberg, "Risk, Ambiguity, and the Savage Axioms," *Quarterly Journal of Economics* 75, no. 4 (1961): 643–99.

71. As he told me in a private conversation, 2 September 2018.

72. Lexicographical order, as its name indicates, is that of the words in a dictionary. The weight of the first letter is infinite in relation to that of the second letter, which itself is infinite in relation to that of the following letter, and so on. Thus the word *axe* comes before *bet*, which comes before *bib*, even though the letter *x* comes after *e*, and *b* comes before *t*.

73. See Rawls, *Theory of Justice*, 42–44, 60–63.

74. For example, randomly choosing a real number between 0 and 1.

75. See Steven P. Lee, "What's Living and What's Dead in Nuclear Ethics? ," in *Ethics and the Future of Conflict: Lessons from the 1990s*, ed. Anthony Lang, Albert Pierce, and Joel Rosenthal (Englewood Cliffs, N.J.: Prentice-Hall, 2004), 91–106.

76. This singular fact cannot be emphasized often enough; so blinding is

the revelation it conveys that it goes unnoticed. MAD has no positive effect. Its only purpose is to prevent its own failure to work.

77. See Schell, *The Abolition*, 153, 181–84. Schell differs from Lee in considering unarmed deterrence to be superior to armed deterrence.

78. The Global Zero Initiative, founded in Paris in 2008, aims to rid the world of nuclear weapons by influencing leaders and governments throughout the world. Its French members include Paul Quilès, a former defense minister under François Mitterrand, and General Bernard Norlain, military advisor to prime ministers Jacques Chirac and Michel Rocard. In 2016, Quilès and Norlain founded the Initiative for Nuclear Disarmament to promote the same objective in France.

79. See the appendix.

80. Girard built his theory of the sacred, and its ambivalent character, on the anthropological evidence of traditional societies dominated by religious belief and practice. In these societies, he maintains, the self-externalization of violence assumes the form of a mechanism that transforms the victim of a crowd's fury into a divinity, at once threatening and protective. Girard tended to minimize the importance of the self-externalization of violence in modern societies, more or less desacralized as a result of the destabilizing effects of the revelation transmitted by the Gospels—hence the apocalyptic pessimism of his last major work, written in collaboration with Benoît Chantre, *Achever Clausewitz* (Paris: Carnets Nord, 2007) and available in English as *Battling to the End*, trans. Mary Baker (East Lansing: Michigan State University Press, 2009). Lee's argument concerning the permanence of MAD in the post-Hiroshima history of humanity can be seen either as confirming Girard's general thesis (and all the more as Lee frankly admits the religious inspiration of his analysis) or as a refutation of Girard's eschatology insofar as MAD appears to be endowed after all with a certain stability—on the edge of the abyss. See my chapter "The Nuclear Menace: A New Sacrament for Humanity," in Jean-Pierre Dupuy, *The Mark of the Sacred* [2008], trans. M. B. DeBevoise (Stanford, Calif.: Stanford University Press, 2013), 175–94.

81. If I may be forgiven for harping on the analogy with quantum mechanics, allow me to point out a parallel here with the theory of decoherence, for example, which accounts for the transition from the quantum state of superposition to a classical state. In this case the equivalent of the act of observation that brings about the quantum transition is the highly enigmatic passage from the indeterminacy of the future to the determination of the present. These considerations take us well beyond the scope of the present volume, however.

82. See in particular Günther Anders, *Die atomare Drohung: Radikale Überlegungen zum atomaren Zeitalter* (Munich: Beck, 1981); also my introduction to the French edition of *Hiroshima ist überall*.

83. See the appendix.

84. Here again the conclusions I have reached call to mind current debates regarding the philosophical foundations of quantum mechanics, especially in relation to the theory of decoherence. See Bernard d'Espagnat and Hervé Zwirn, eds., *Les débats philosophiques de la physique quantique* (Paris: Éditions Matériologiques, 2014).

85. I am pleased to have arrived at this conclusion jointly with the historian Barton Bernstein, a foremost expert. Private conversation, Stanford, 17 August 2017.

Appendix

1. Thérèse Delpech, in *La dissuasion nucléaire au XXIe siècle* (Paris: Odile Jacob, 2012), summarily dismisses game theory. She says, for example, that it is not clear "why 'moves' [in a game] must be formalized in order to be understood and what all this has to do with everyday decision-making." There are two things she does not grasp. First, that game theory and, more generally, the theory of rational choice are interesting precisely because, *owing to their inadequacy*, they cast light on the very elements of the nuclear "game" that escape the narrow rationality postulated by these theories; second, that this type of formulation aims not at modeling real phenomena but at clarifying concepts—for example, the concept of deterrence—that remain vaguely defined in journalistic and other popularizing accounts.

2. See Jorge Luis Borges, "The Garden of Forking Paths" [1941], trans. Helen Temple and Ruthven Todd, in *Ficciones* (New York: Grove Press, 1962), 89–101. David K. Lewis refers to this story in an article on "time's arrow," one of the most profound pleadings on behalf of what I call the orthodox conception of time, which is to say occurring time; see "Counterfactual Dependence and Time's Arrow," *Noûs* 13, no. 4 (1979): 455–76, reprinted with postscripts in *Philosophical Papers*, 2 vols. (New York: Oxford University Press, 1983–1986), 2:32–66.

3. See David P. Gauthier, *Morals by Agreement* (Oxford: Clarendon Press, 1986); also, on the nuclear question, David P. Gauthier, "Deterrence, Maximization, and Rationality," *Ethics* 94, no. 3 (1984): 474–95.

4. See Jean-Pierre Dupuy, "Philosophical Foundations of a New Concept of Equilibrium in the Social Sciences: Projected Equilibrium," *Philosophical Studies* 100 (2000): 323–45.

5. For a good introduction to this game, and particularly to the complicated history of its discovery and subsequent elaboration as well as the origin of the game's name, see William Poundstone, *The Prisoner's Dilemma: John von Neumann, Game Theory, and the Puzzle of the Bomb* (New York: Doubleday, 1992).

6. Thomas Hobbes, ch. 11, *Leviathan, or the Matter, Forme, & Power of a Common-Wealth Ecclesiastical and Civill* (London, 1651). François Tricaud, the brilliant French translator of *Leviathan*, rendered *anticipation* as "prendre les devants," which is to say "to act first, to preempt."

7. The best illustration of the prisoner's dilemma, well before it was formalized in 1950 by two mathematicians working at RAND, Merrill Flood and Melvin Dresher, is found in the 1782 novel by the French artillery officer Pierre Choderlos de Laclos, *Les Liaisons dangereuses*. In her letter of 4 December 17** to the Vicomte de Valmont, the Marquise de Merteuil writes this:

> Let us consider what is all this ado about. You found Danceny with me, and it displeased you? Well and good: but what conclusion can you have drawn from it? Either it was the result of chance, as I told you, or of my will, as I did not tell you. In the first case, your letter is unjust; in the second, it is ridiculous: it was indeed worth the trouble of writing! But you are jealous, and jealousy does not reason. Very well, let me reason for you. Either you have a rival or you have not. If you have one, you must please, in order to be preferred to him; if you have not, you must still please, in order to avoid having one. In both cases the same conduct is to be observed: why, therefore, torment yourself? Above all, why torment me? Do you no longer know how to be the most amiable? And are you no longer sure of your successes? Come now, Vicomte, you do yourself an injustice." (Trans. Ernest Dowson [London: Leonard Smithers, 1898])

The Marquise de Merteuil's reasoning brings out in a striking way the apparently implacable logic of a dominant strategy. "In both cases the same conduct is to be observed": the best choice is clear, there is no reason to torment oneself. Uncertainty about the situation in no way affects the decision that should be made, since this decision is independent of the situation. The prisoner's dilemma brings two dominant strategies, one for each agent, into conflict, and this conflict is disastrous for both of them.

8. See ch. 3, n. 15.

9. These are Nash equilibria. In such an equilibrium, by definition, each player maximizes his payoff by supposing that the other's action is fixed, which is to say counterfactually independent of his own action. Obviously there exists a third non-catastrophic state, the square (r, r), in which both rivals swerve at the same time, as we all do in ordinary driving situations without feeling at all humiliated. But this is not an equilibrium, for by swerving, each allows the other player to remain in the middle of the road.

10. Bernard Brodie, *War and Politics* (New York: Macmillan, 1973), 430–31; the emphasis is mine.

11. Alison McQueen, in her excellent book *Political Realism in Apocalyptic Times* (New York: Cambridge University Press, 2018), studies the

political thought of Machiavelli and Hobbes in relation to that of Hans Morgenthau, a German Jewish émigré who came to the United States in 1932. Under the influence of both the memory of the Shoah and the anticipation of nuclear apocalypse, Morgenthau went on to play an important part in the rise of realism in the theory of international relations after World War II. Citing my own work, McQueen sees Morgenthau as having relied on self-defeating prophecy in the following sense: the imminent occurrence of a nuclear apocalypse needs to be predicted as if it were an ineluctable fatality, with the aim of preventing its occurrence by the very fact of the prophecy. From this it will be clear that the solution I propose does not imply that the prophet of doom need be a false prophet, as I go on to show.

12. I use the word *actual* in its philosophical sense, in English as in Latin: of all possible worlds, the one that is realized.

13. Note that (Alter, r; Ego, R) is a Nash equilibrium for the game in question. It is an *imperfect* Nash equilibrium, however, in the sense that it is not supported by a credible threat.

14. This involves a backtracking counterfactual conditional of the type "If I were to buy an apartment on the Avenue Foch in Paris, it is because I am rich." Compare this to: "If I were to buy an apartment on the Avenue Foch in Paris, I would be poor" (since bankrupt as a result).

15. The title I gave this appendix in the French edition, "Jeux nucléaires, jeux interdits," has a double meaning: on the one hand, these games, whether they assume the form of the prisoner's dilemma or the game of chicken, are extremely dangerous and it is best not to tempt the devil; on the other hand, in projected time, certain moves are prohibited, such as (Ego, R), for they are causally ruled out by the past, which anticipates them.

Acknowledgments

1. Very few leading French intellectuals have troubled themselves to inquire into the question of nuclear war. Albert Camus's editorial in the immediate aftermath of Hiroshima is often quoted: "Mechanical civilization has just reached the height of its savagery. It will soon be necessary to choose, in the more or less near future, between collective suicide and the intelligent use of scientific discoveries" (*Combats*, 8 August 1945)—a prescient insight, going against the almost universal enthusiasm of the period, but hardly a substitute for rigorous analysis. Raymond Aron's two-volume study of Clausewitz (Gallimard, 1976) is a very fine work, but his engrained rationalism prevented him from understanding the madness of nuclear reason. René Girard's final book, *Achever Clausewitz* (Carnets Nord, 2007), by contrast, even though it has little to say about nuclear warfare, has been a major source of inspiration to me.